The "Gadget Book"
A Tool for Creative People

by

J. Ronald Adair

Published by

ELTEK Publishing

V 1.01

Introduction

> **gadget**
>
> (ˈgædʒɪt)
>
> *n*
>
> **1.** a small mechanical device or appliance
> **2.** any object that is interesting for its ingenuity or novelty rather than for its practical use

While neither of the above definitions are *exactly* applicable to this book, the overall design of it is definitely novel – and we hope it proves to have practical use also.

Although there are many journals from day planners to coloring books, there seemed to be a need for a journal targeted to a specific group of people. Who are these? They are people on the go, creative, with possible entrepreneurial leanings. Ones that think of new ideas or better ways of doing things. Those that may have an ah-ha moment at any time and need to document it.

The Gadget Book is a way of doing this. It has information areas, drawing panels, doodling or pattern creation pages. The layout will help you to have a recording journal for your creative efforts!

There are multiple 'sets' of panels and pages with the first page being an information page, followed by many interesting patterns to help formulate ideas and plans. The sets may be used on a daily basis, or a range of days. When needed you can progress to the next set.

Thanks for your purchase and good gadgeting!

This Journal is the Property of

____

| Date: | | Day | |

Websites to Note

Need to Purchase

Simple Day Planner

New Contacts-Friends

Project Updates

Books I Want to Remember

Music I Liked

TV/Movies I Liked

Five New Ideas

Social Media Links

Twitter	
Facebook	
Instagram	
Pinterest	
Snapchat	
Other	

Other Notes

Link to Page _________

Description:

[4]

Description:

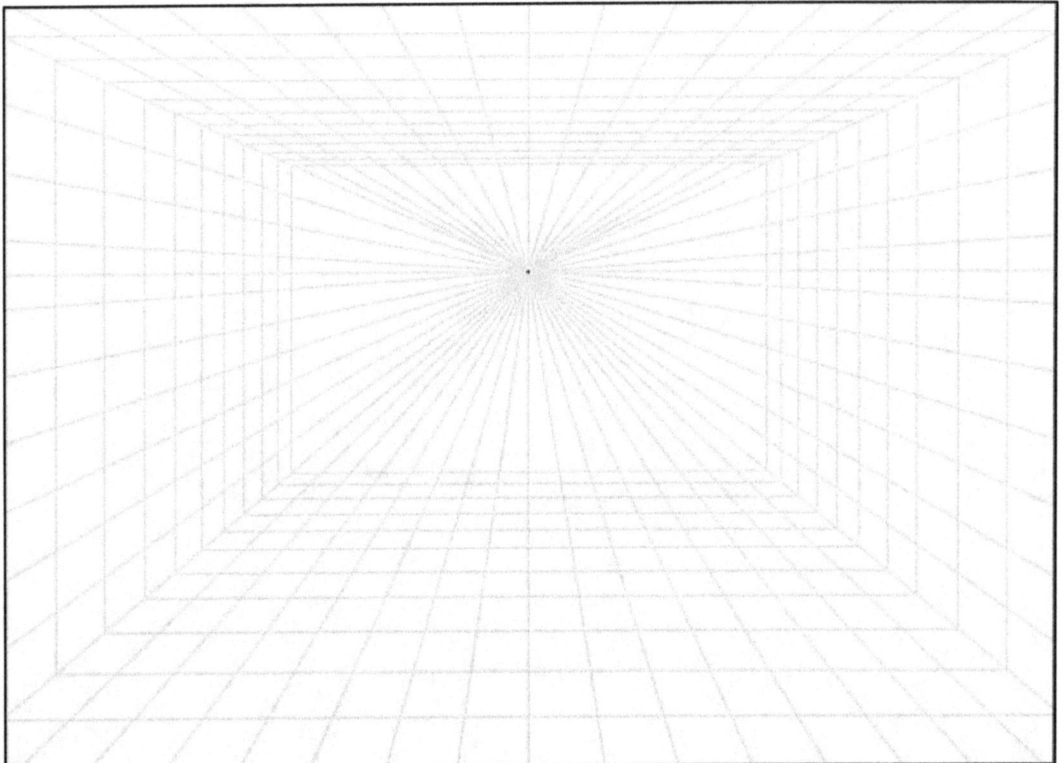

Description:

Description:

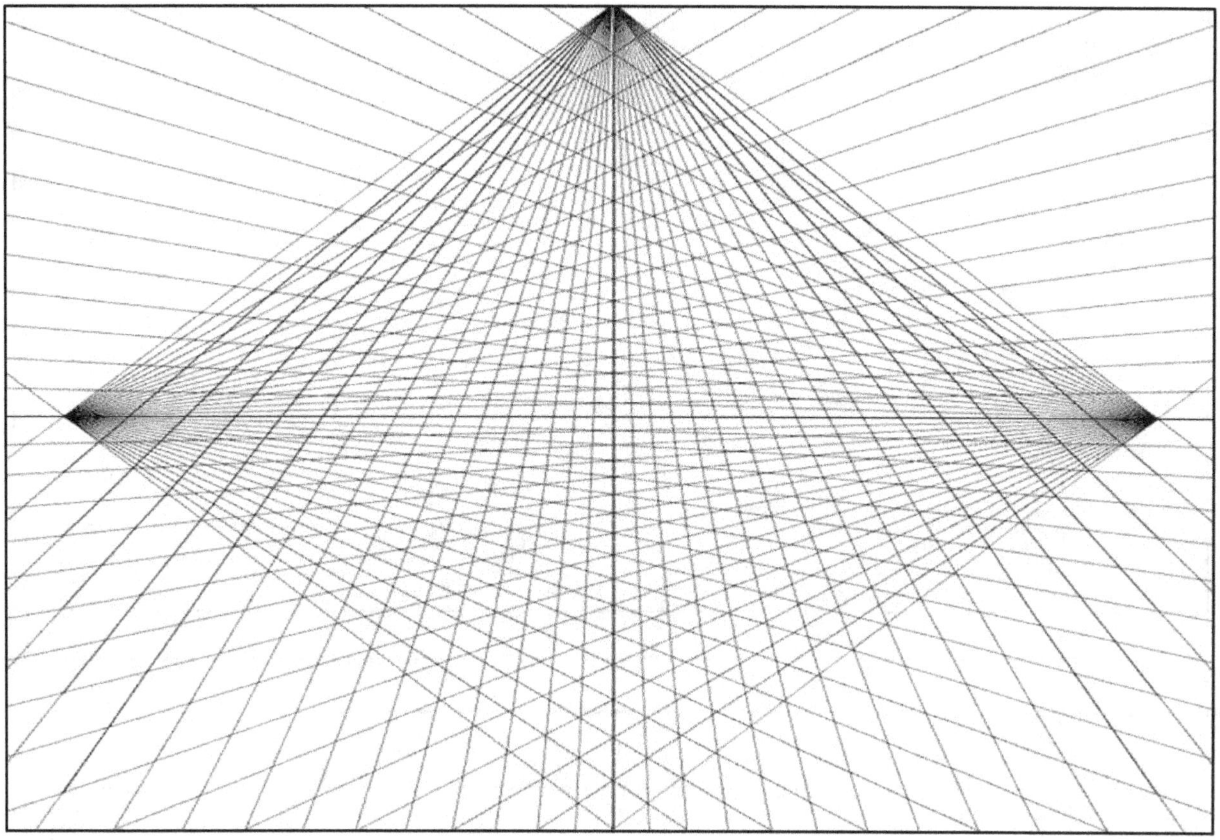

Description:

Description:

Description:

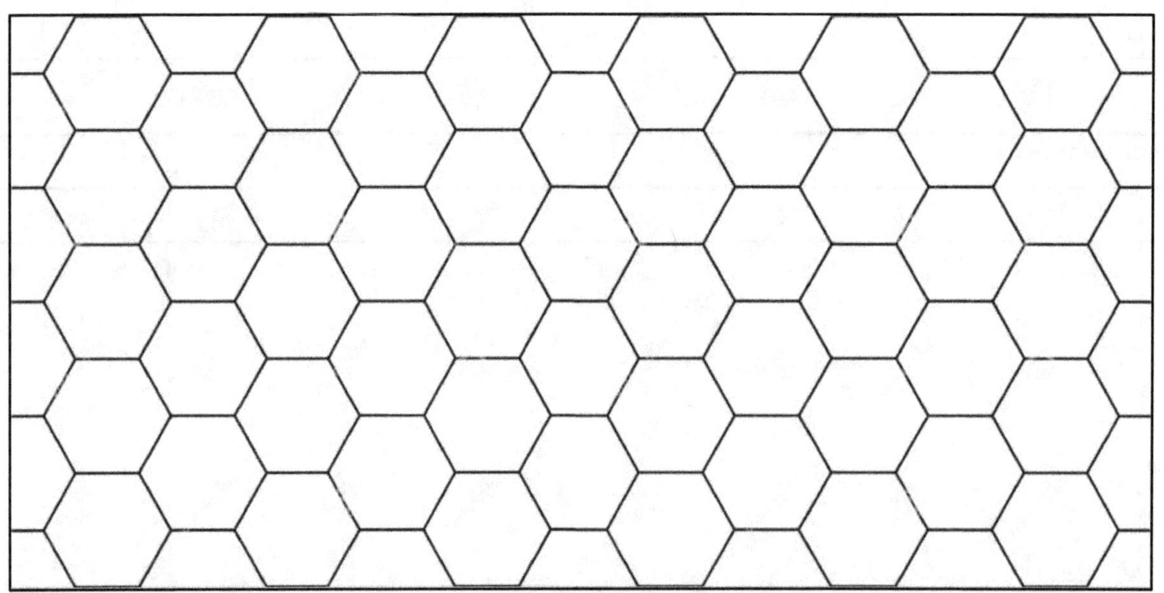

Description:

Description:

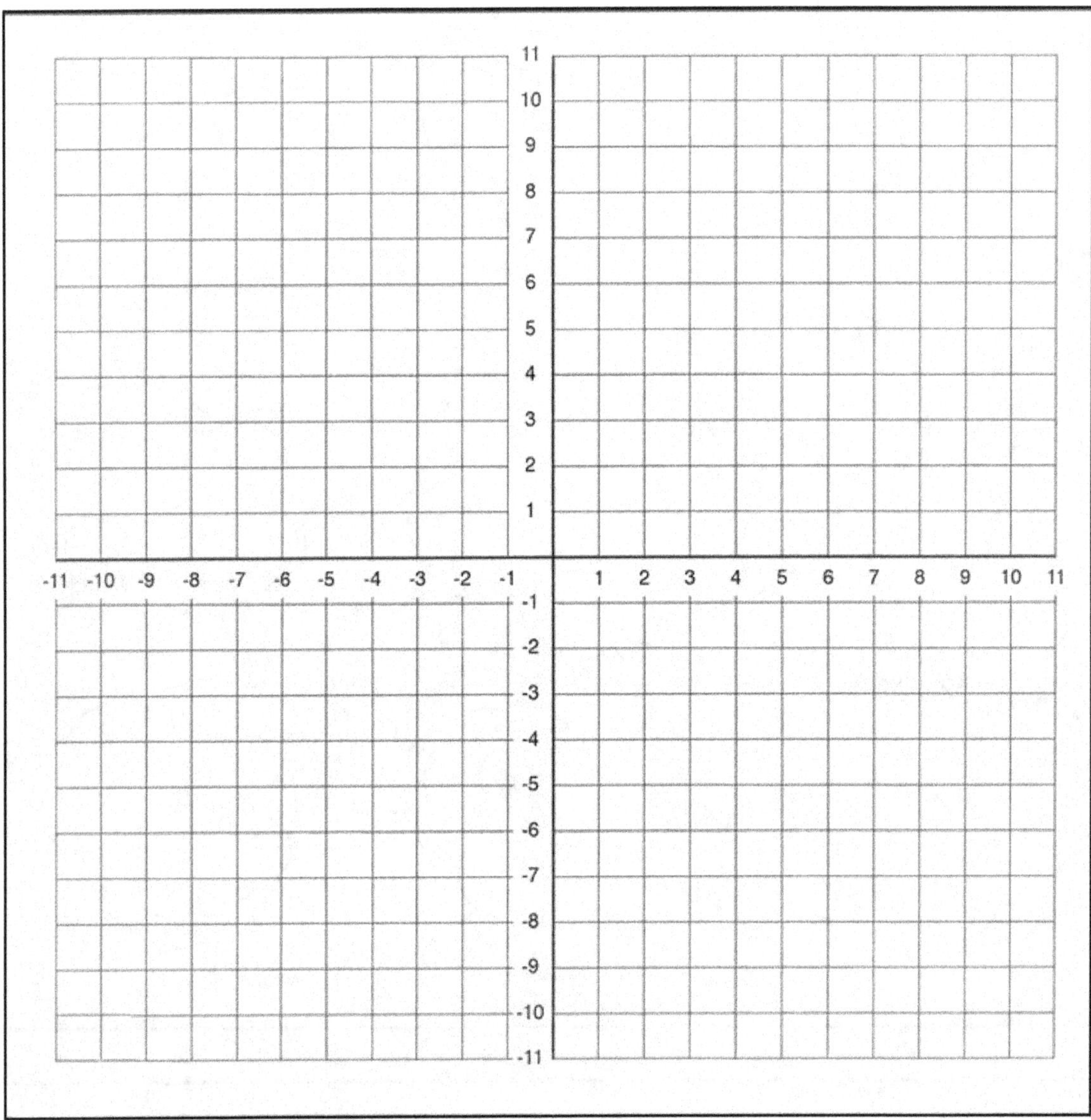

New words or phrases learned today:	Building or architectural design I like:
Ideas from a co-worker or classmate I liked:	Notes:

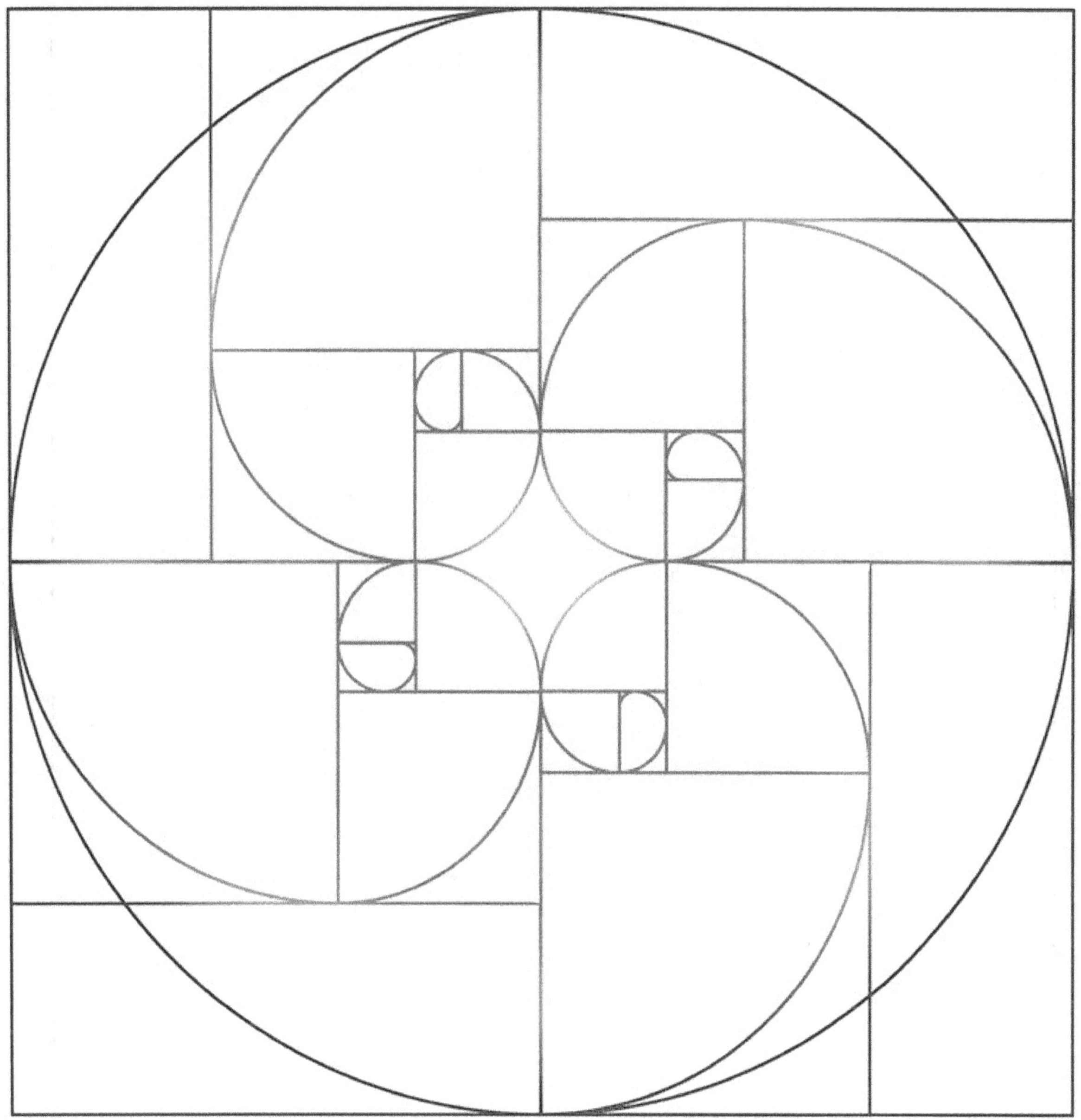

| Date: | | Day | |

Websites to Note

Need to Purchase

Simple Day Planner

New Contacts-Friends

Project Updates

Books I Want to Remember

Music I Liked

TV/Movies I Liked

Five New Ideas

Social Media Links

Twitter	
Facebook	
Instagram	
Pinterest	
Snapchat	
Other	

Other Notes

Link to Page __________

Description:

Description:

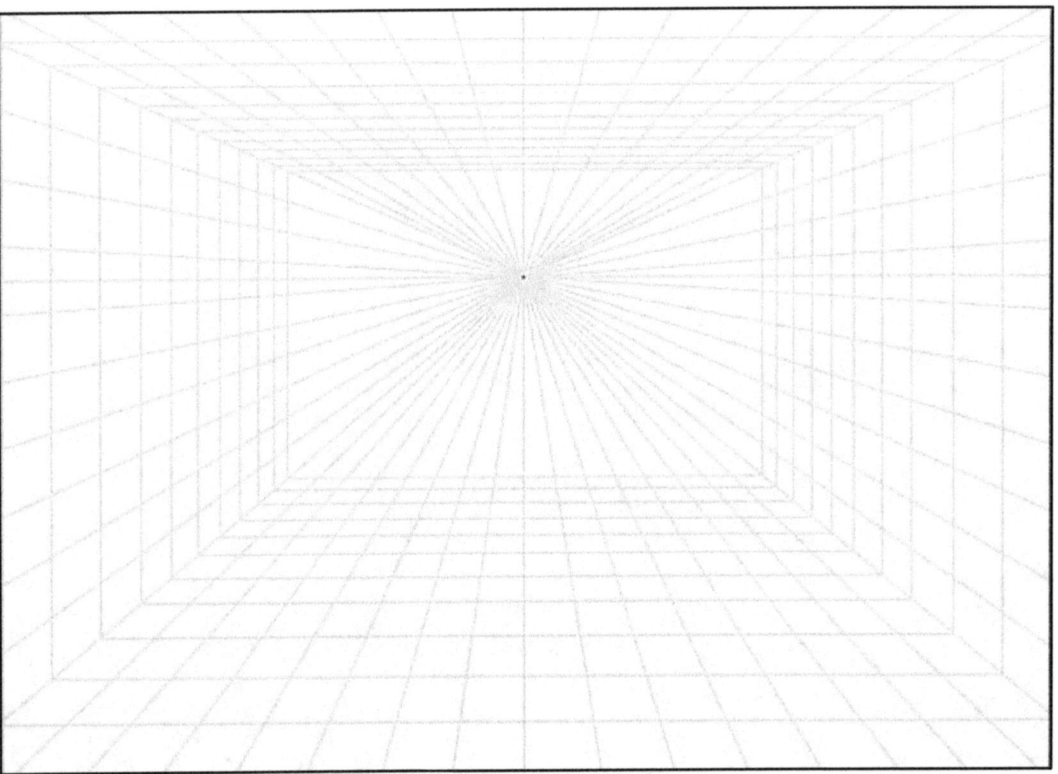

Description:

Description:

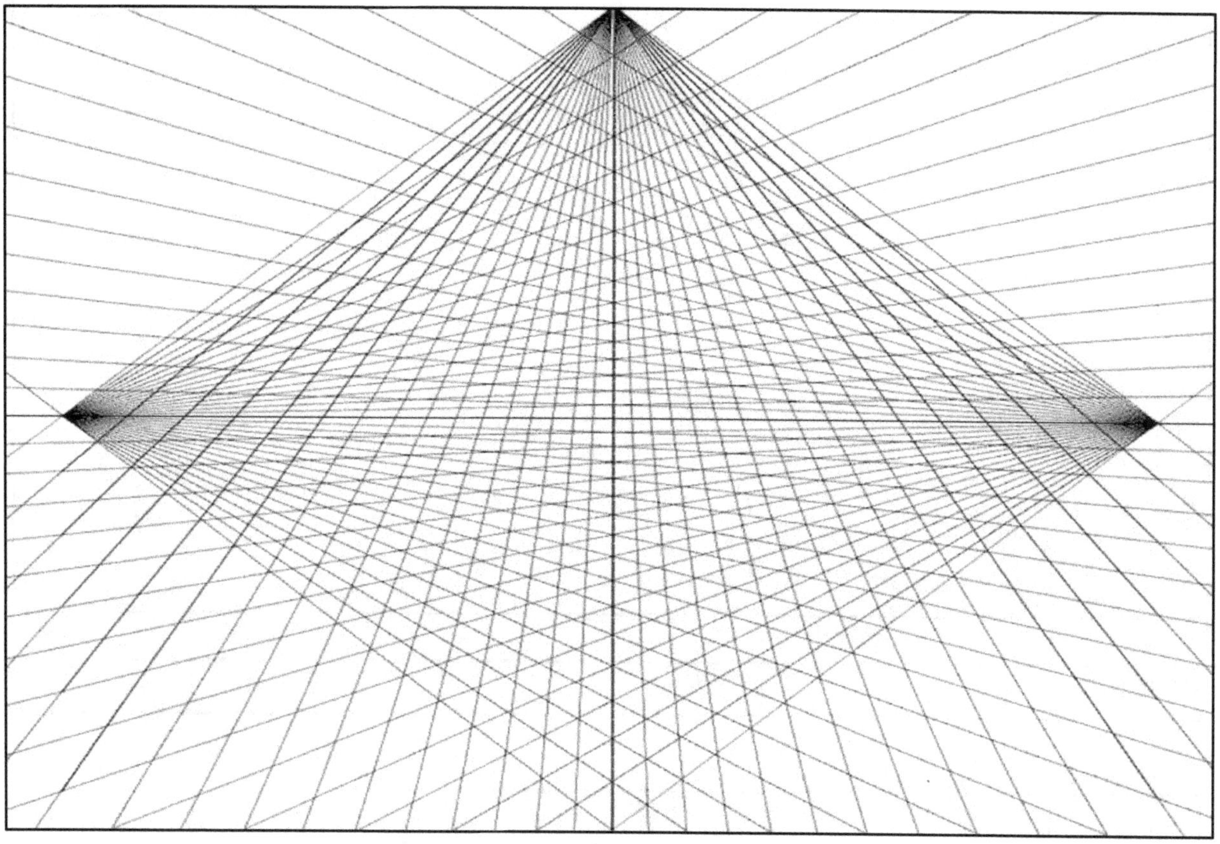

Description:

Description:

Description:

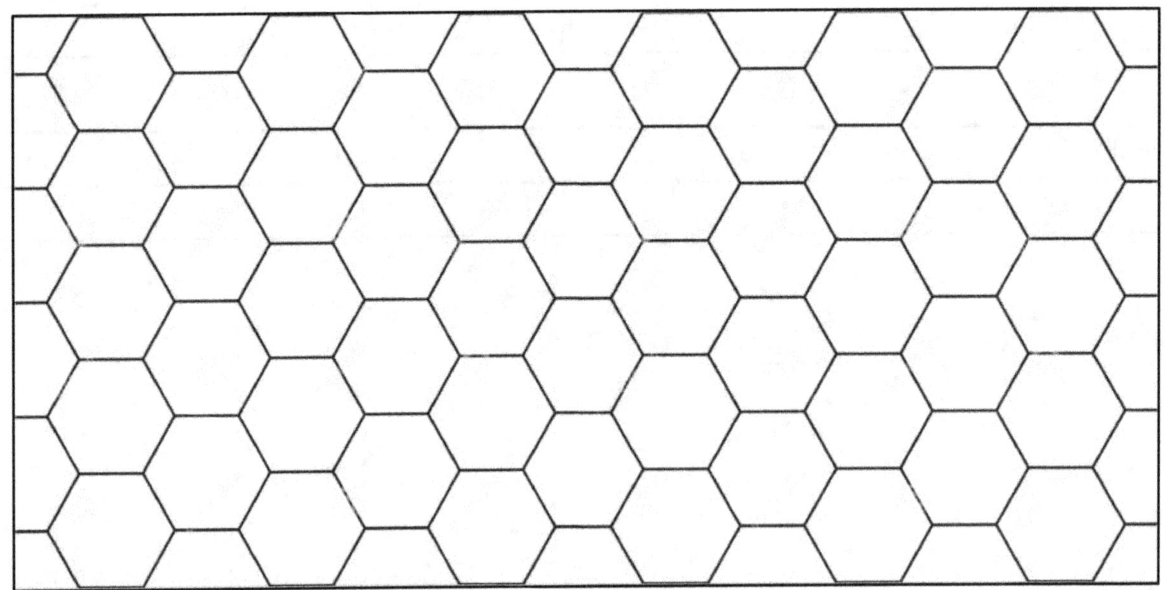

Description:

Description:

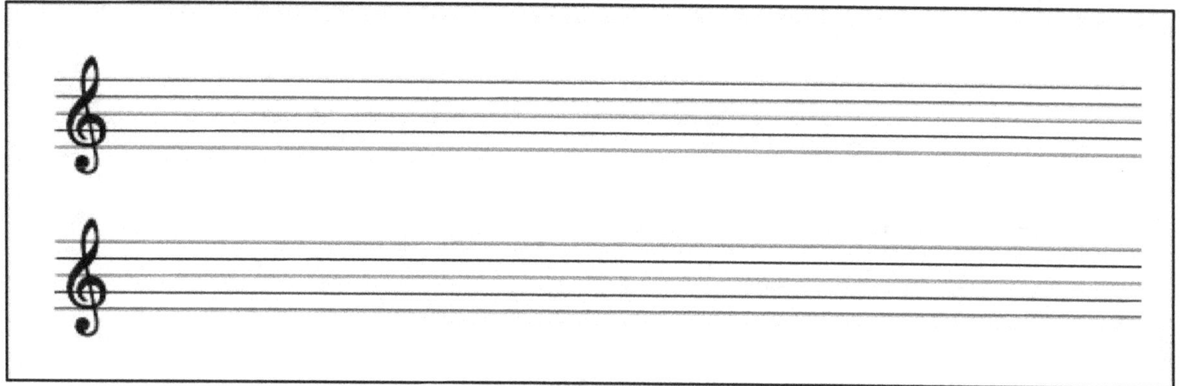

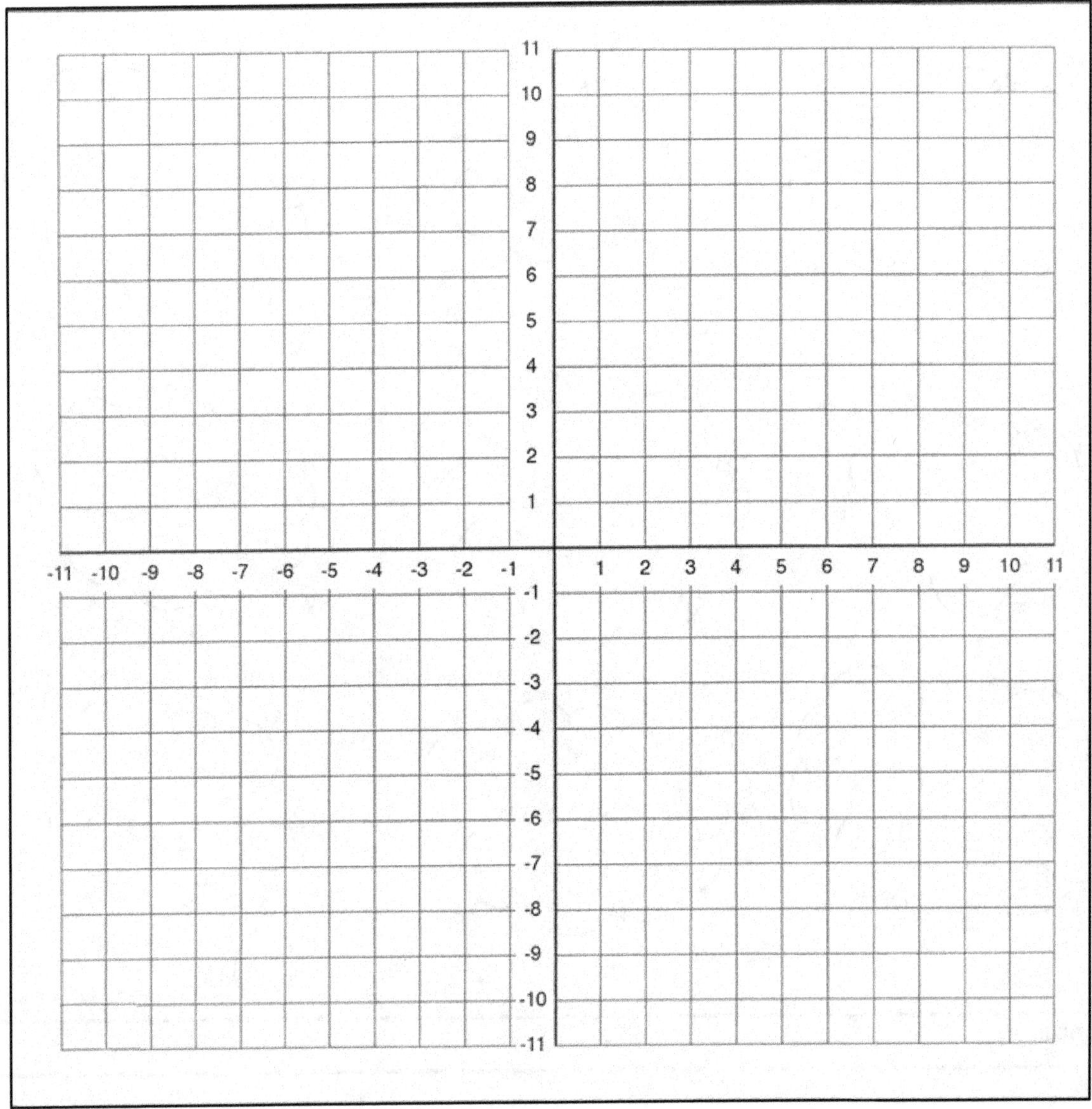

New words or phrases learned today:	Building or architectural design I like:
Ideas from a co-worker or classmate I liked:	Notes:

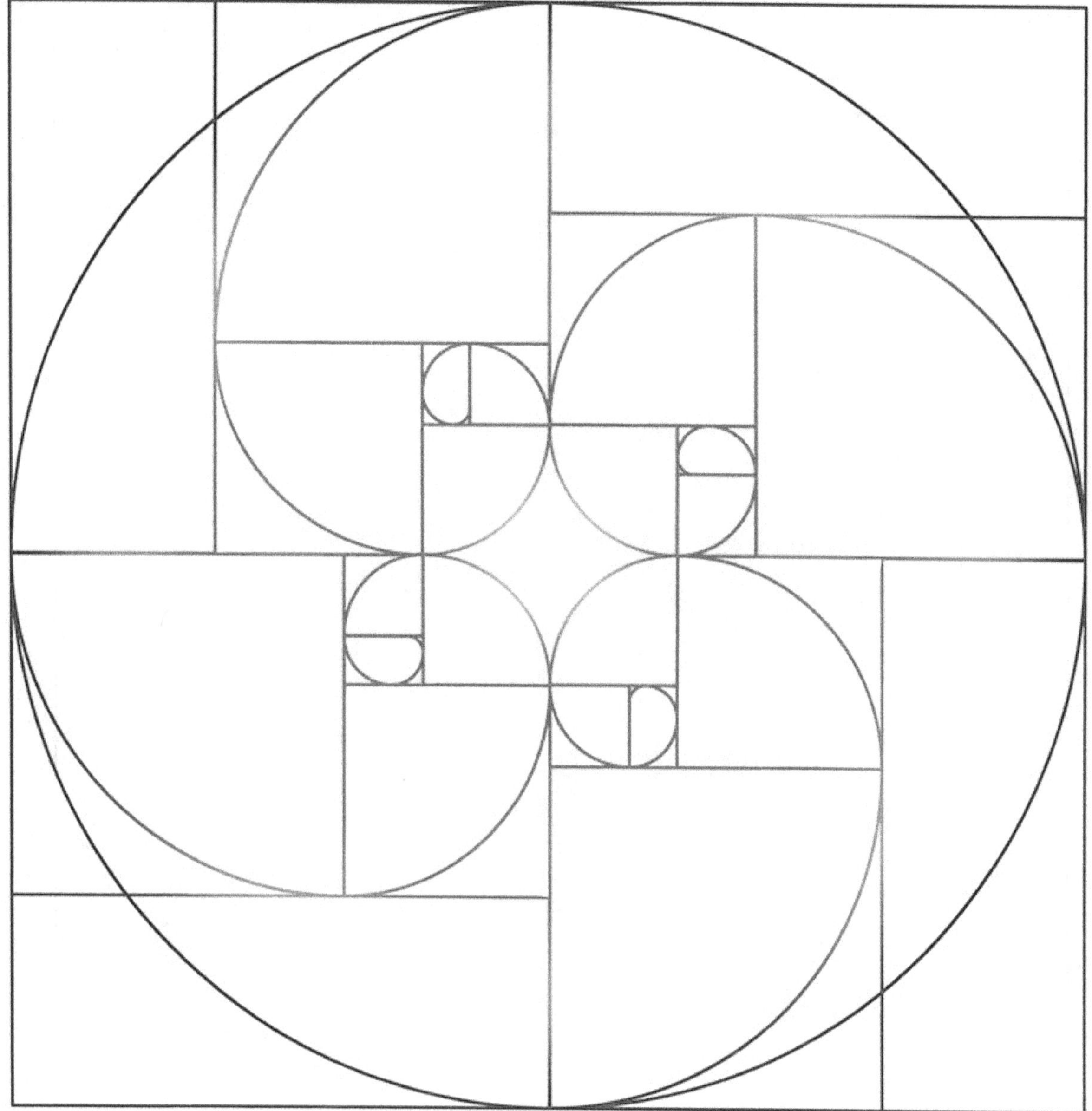

| Date: | | Day | |

Websites to Note

Need to Purchase

Simple Day Planner

New Contacts-Friends

Project Updates

Books I Want to Remember

Music I Liked

TV/Movies I Liked

Five New Ideas

Social Media Links

Twitter	
Facebook	
Instagram	
Pinterest	
Snapchat	
Other	

Other Notes

Link to Page __________

Description:

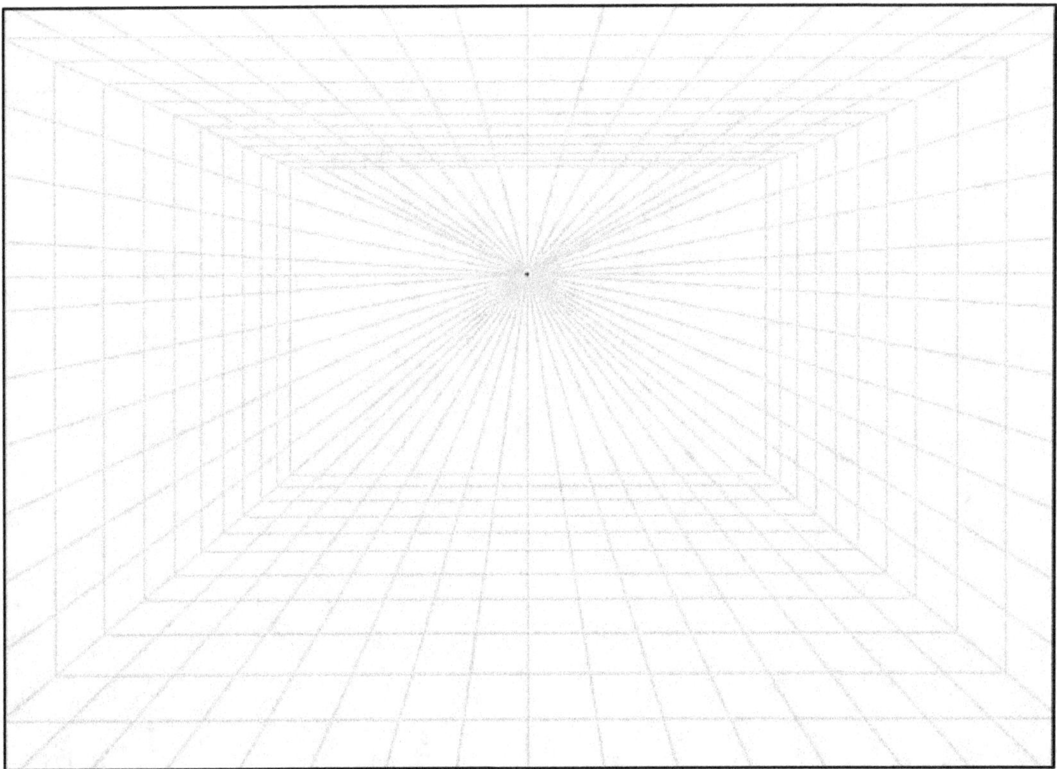

Description:

Description:

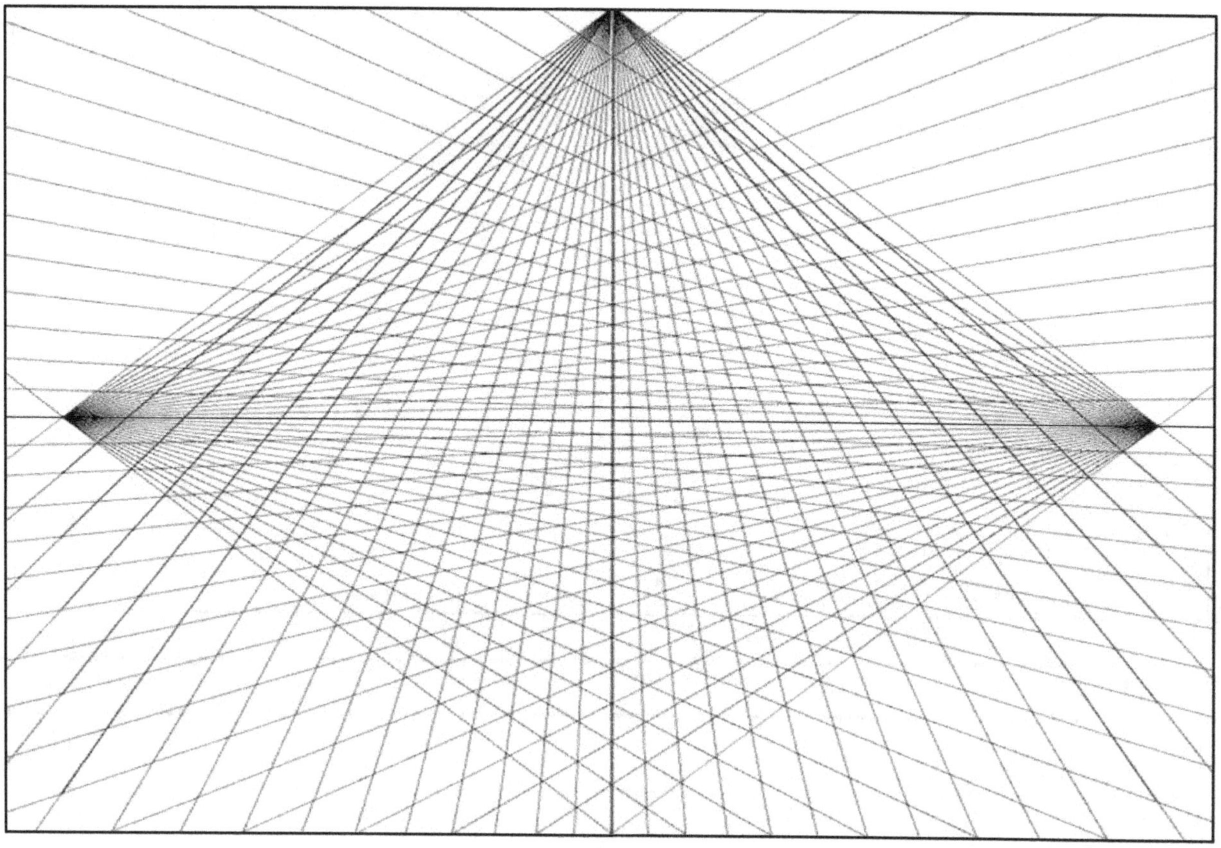

Description:

Description:

Description:

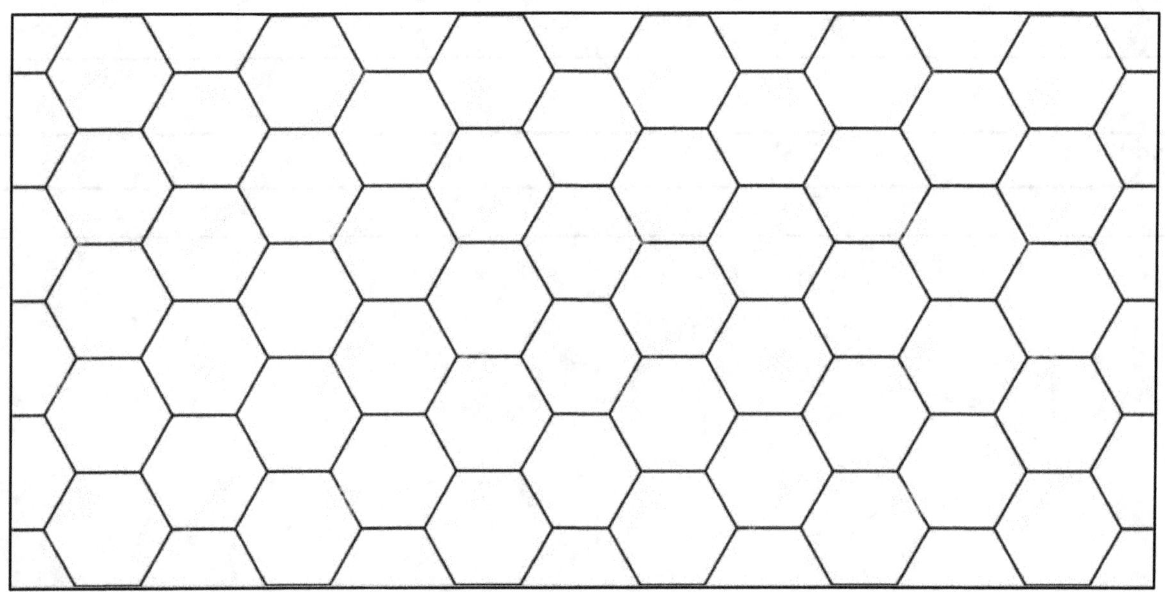

Description:

Description:

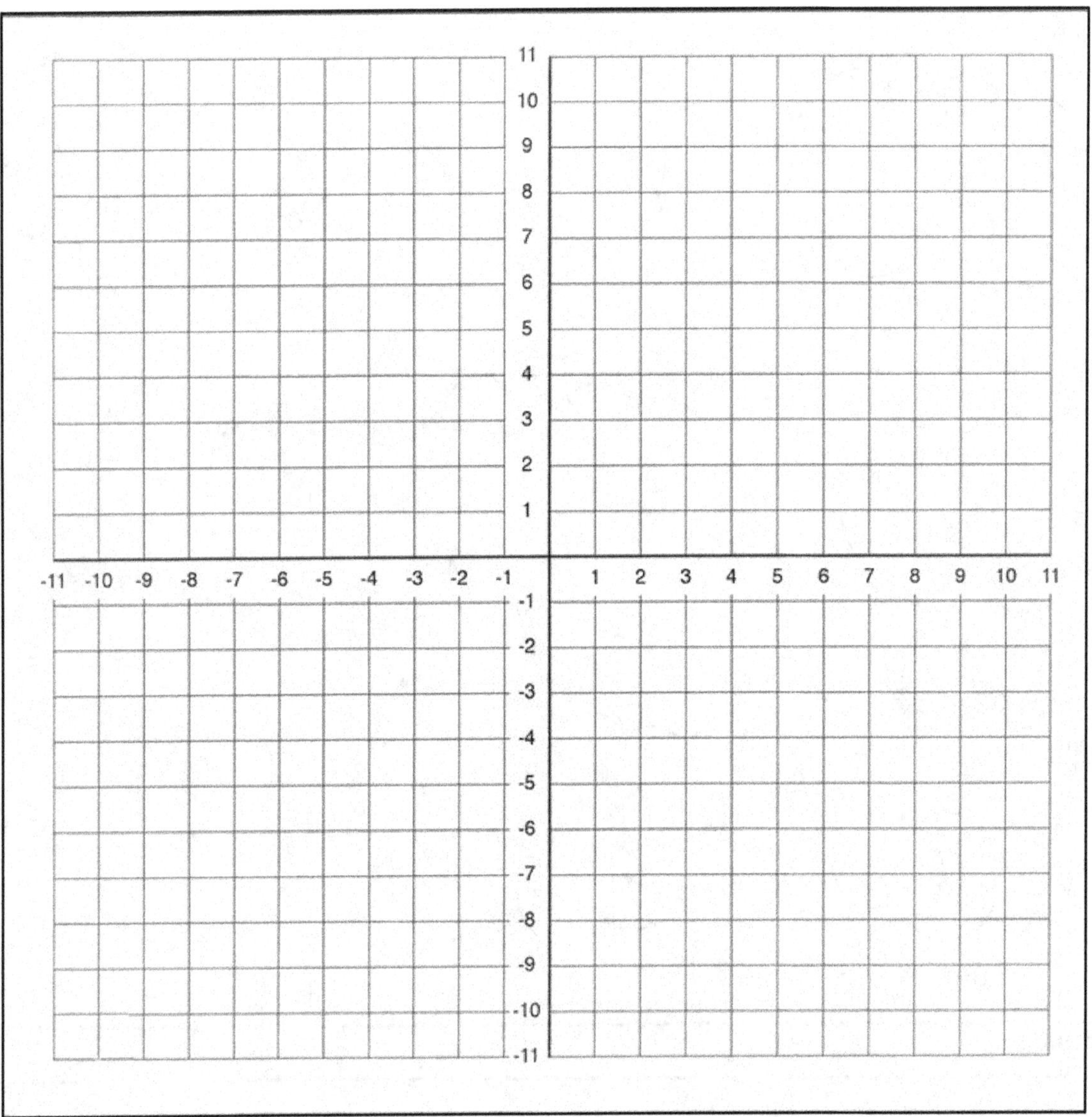

New words or phrases learned today:	Building or architectural design I like:
Ideas from a co-worker or classmate I liked:	Notes:

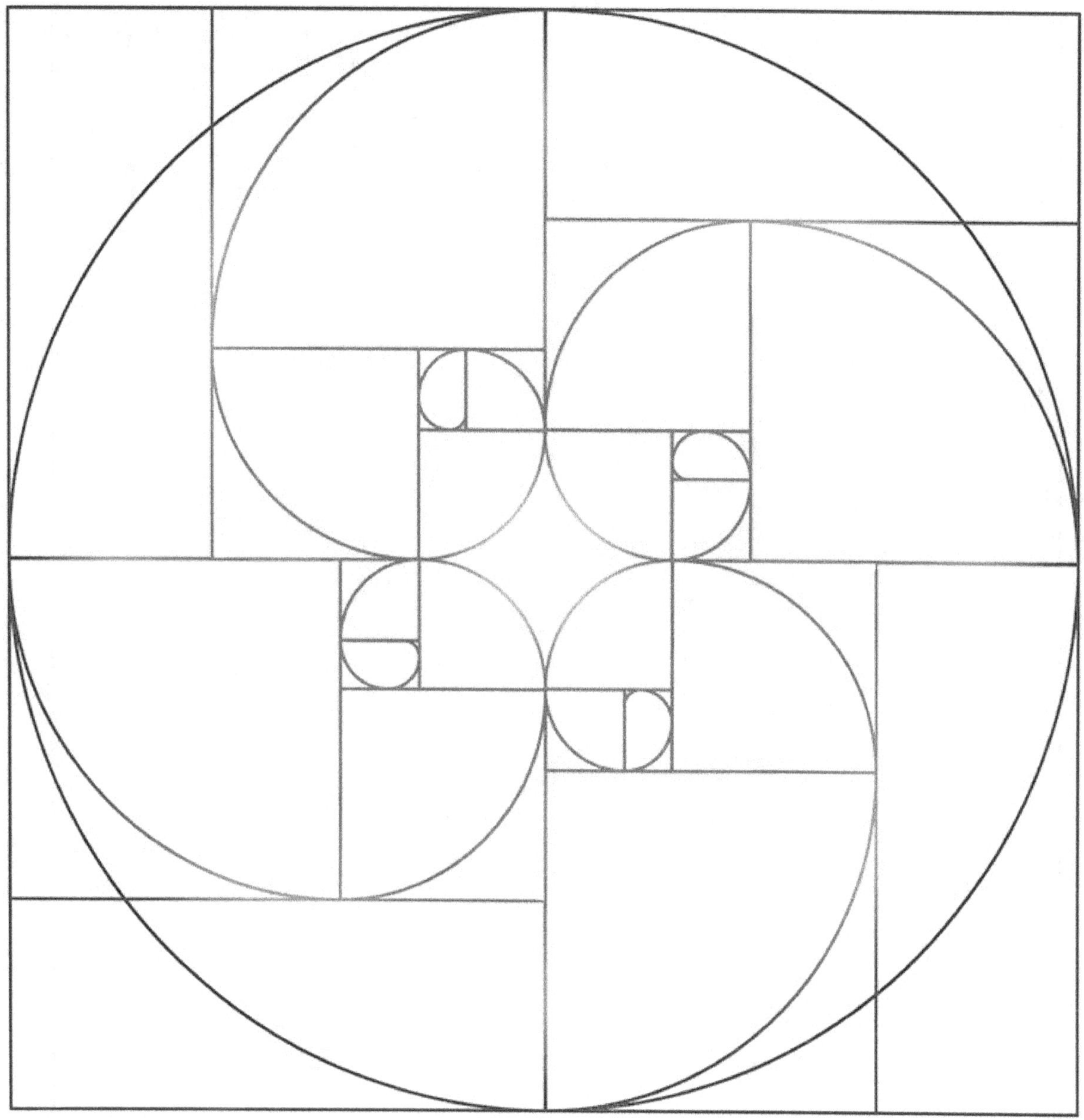

<table>
<tr><td>Date:</td><td></td><td>Day</td><td></td></tr>
</table>

Websites to Note

Need to Purchase

Simple Day Planner

New Contacts-Friends

Project Updates

Books I Want to Remember

Music I Liked

TV/Movies I Liked

Five New Ideas

Social Media Links

Twitter	
Facebook	
Instagram	
Pinterest	
Snapchat	
Other	

Other Notes

Link to Page ________

Description:

Description:

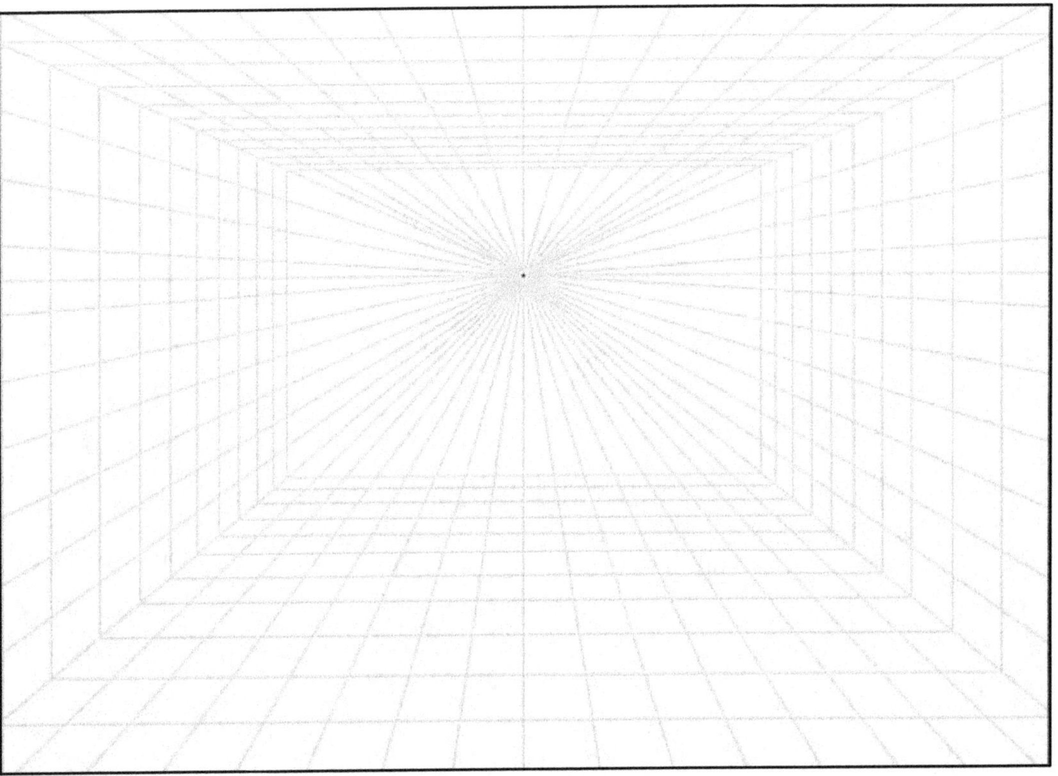

Description:

Description:

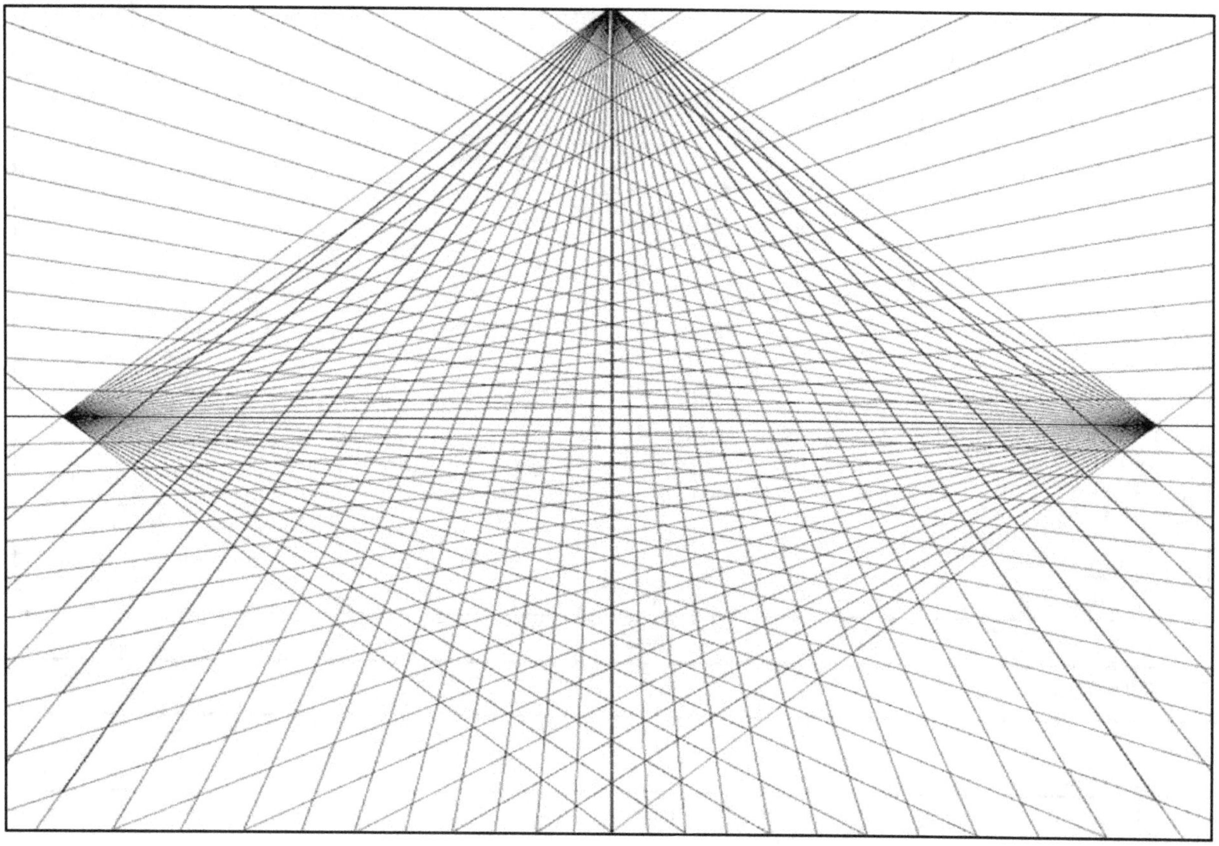

Description:

Description:

Description:

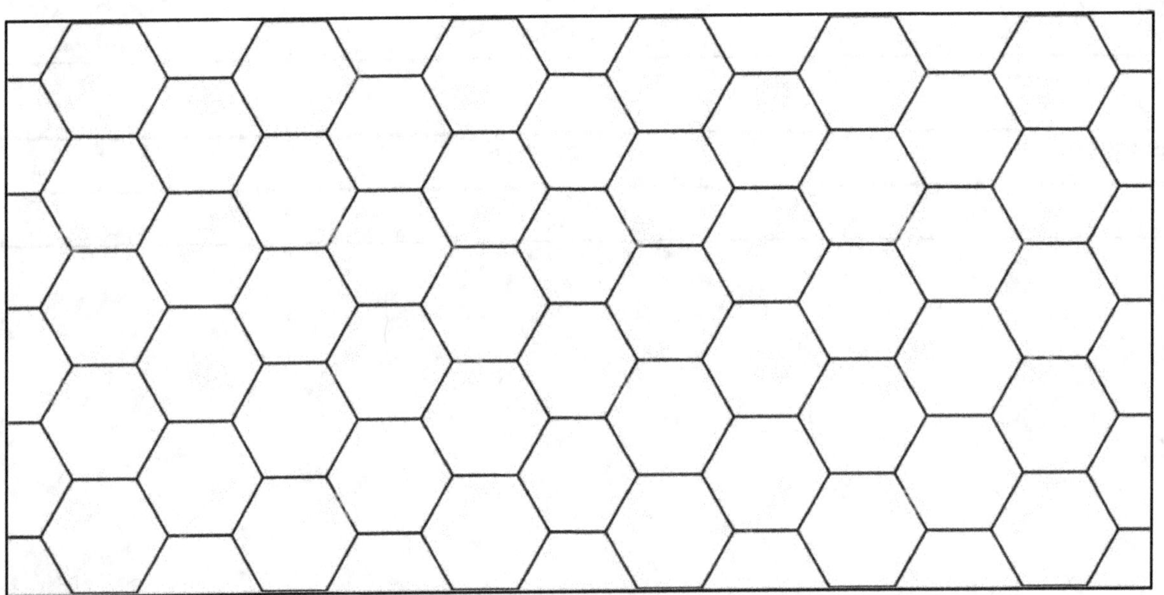

Description:

Description:

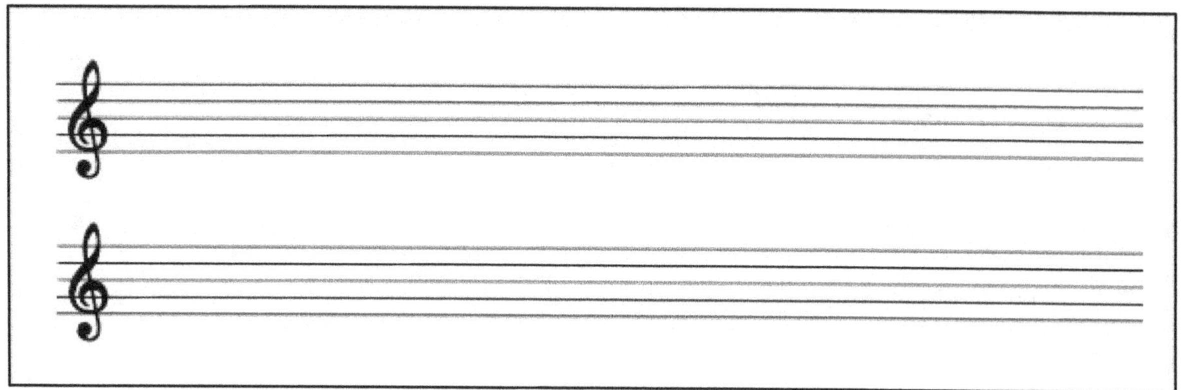

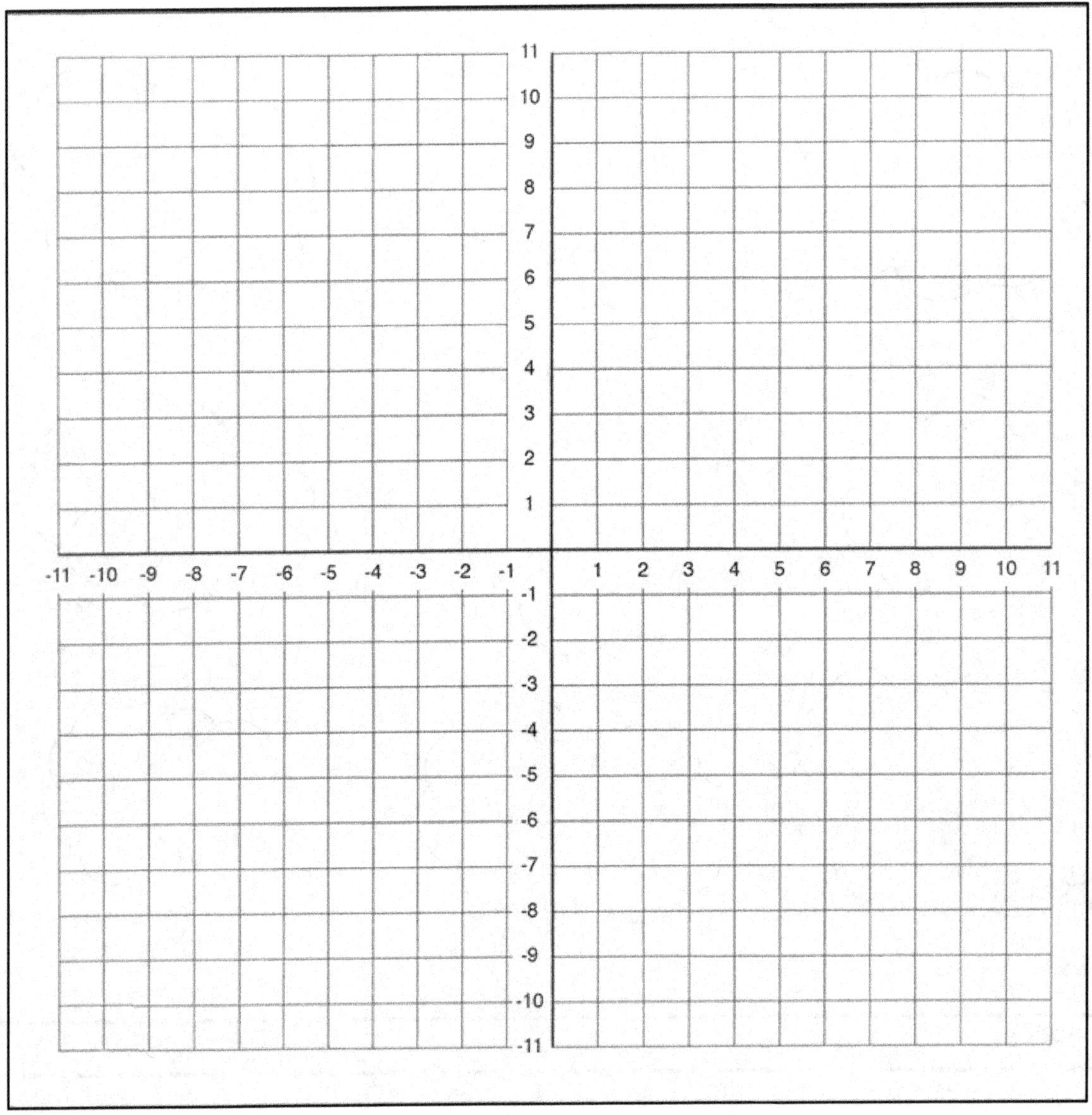

New words or phrases learned today:	Building or architectural design I like:
Ideas from a co-worker or classmate I liked:	Notes:

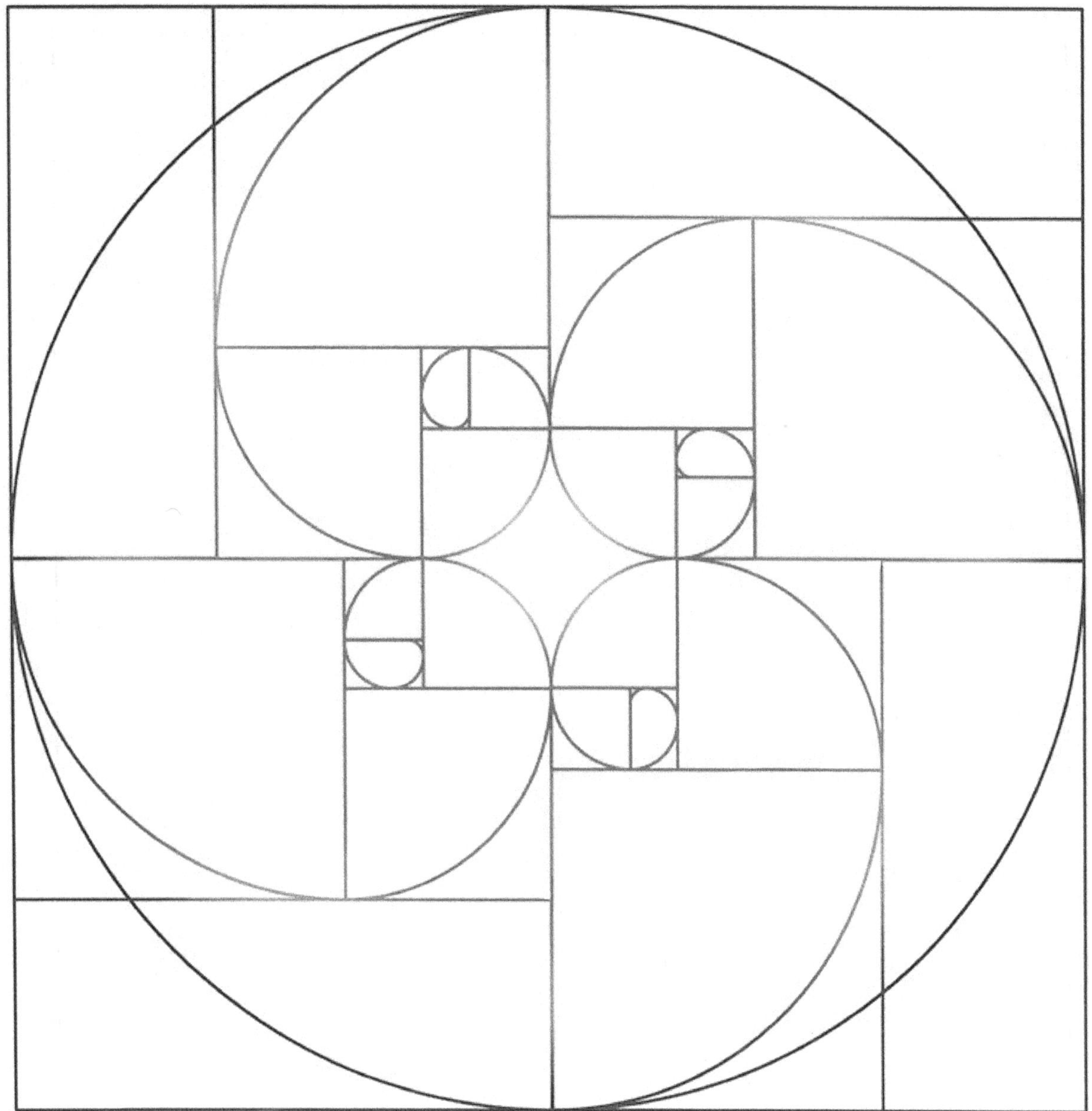

Date:		Day	

Websites to Note

Need to Purchase

Simple Day Planner

New Contacts-Friends

Project Updates

Books I Want to Remember

Music I Liked

TV/Movies I Liked

Five New Ideas

Social Media Links

Twitter	
Facebook	
Instagram	
Pinterest	
Snapchat	
Other	

Other Notes

Link to Page ________

Description:

Description:

Description:

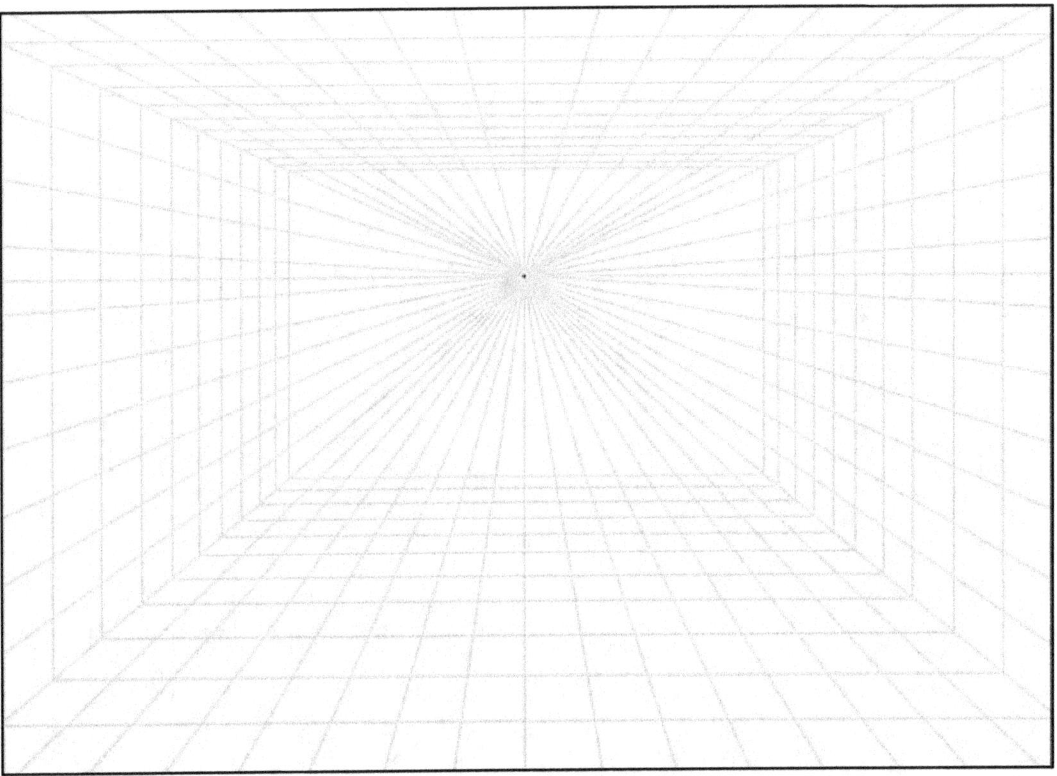

Description:

Description:

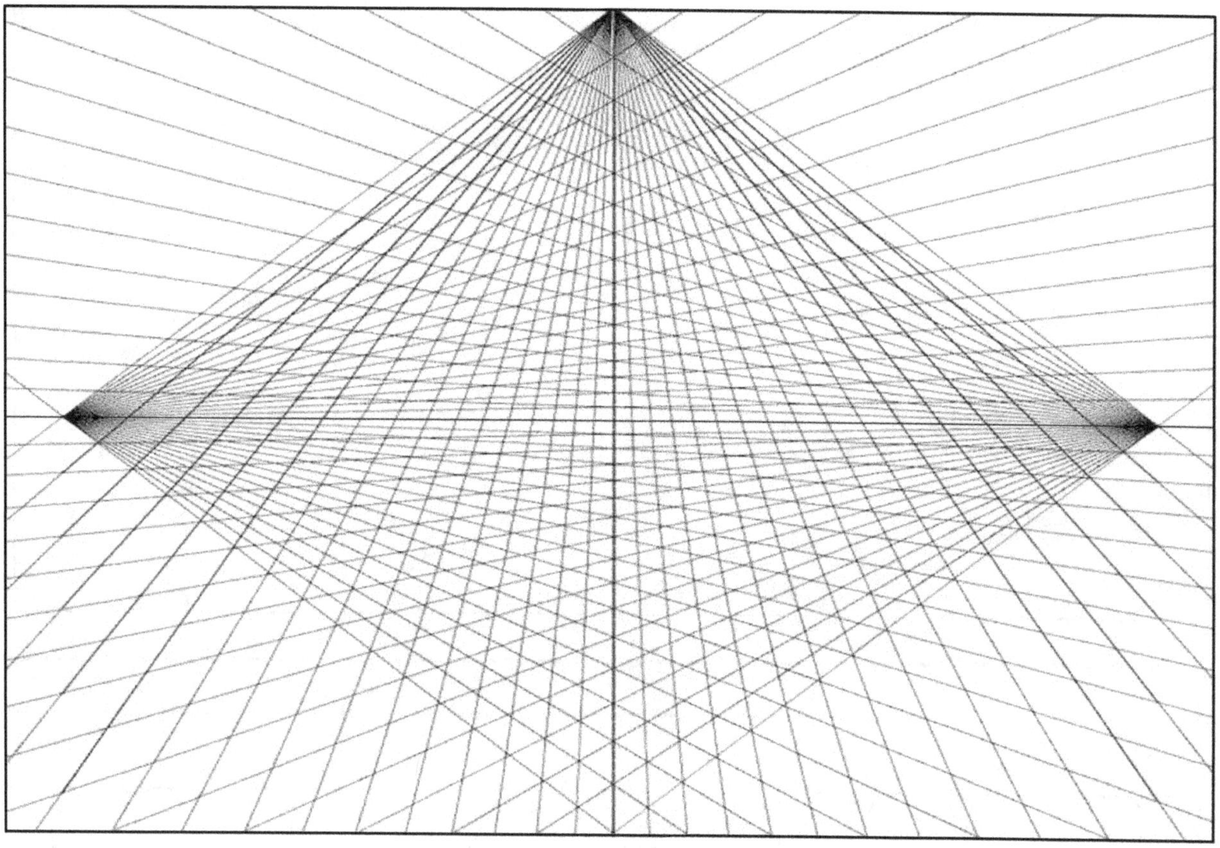

Description:

Description:

Description:

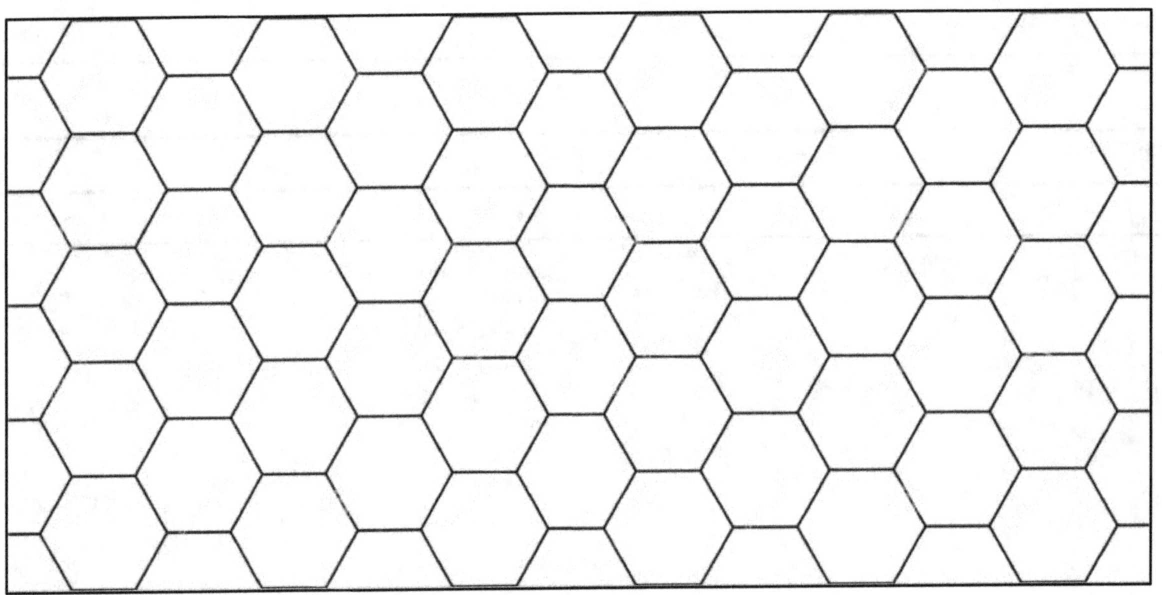

Description:

Description:

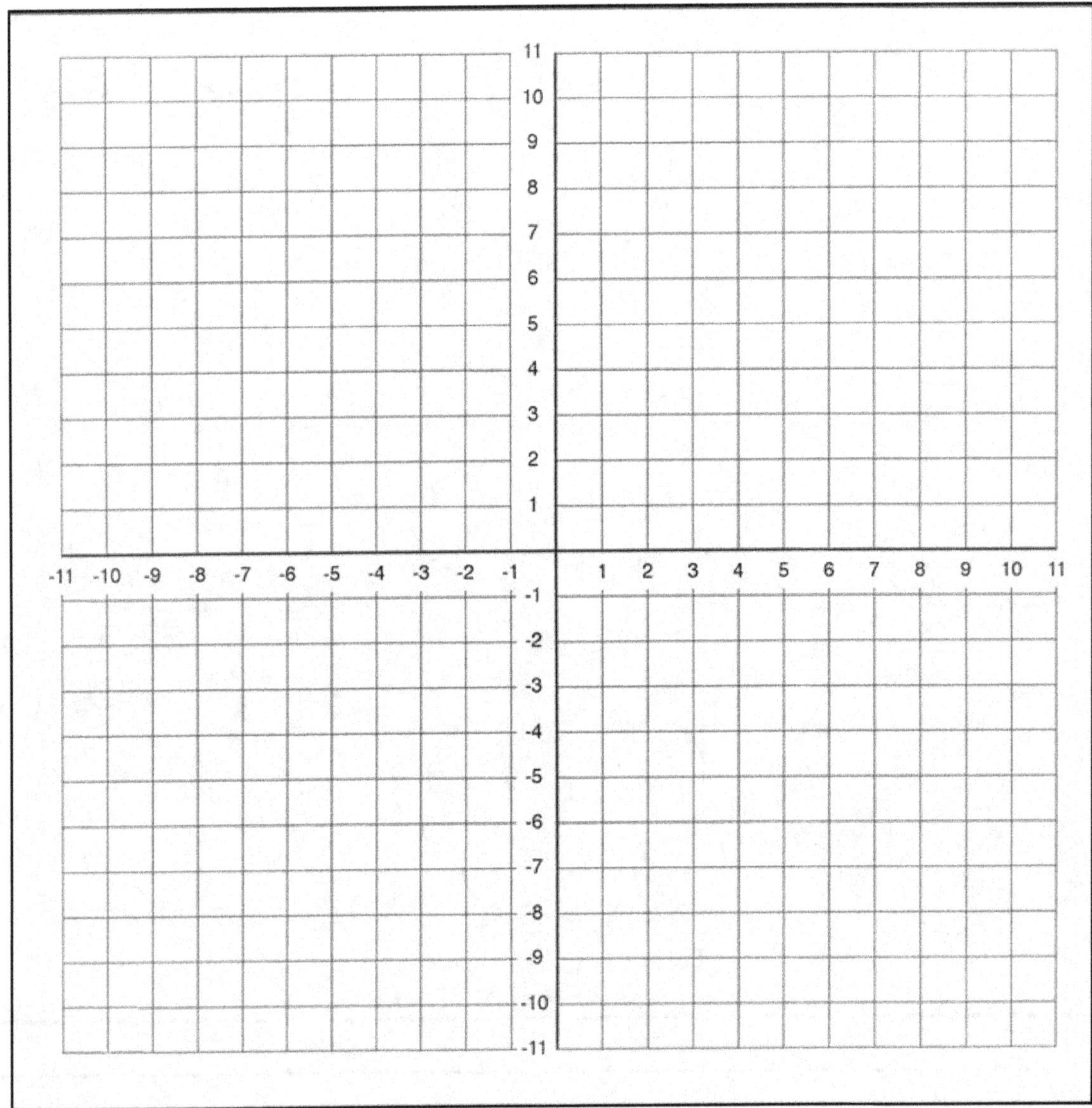

New words or phrases learned today:	Building or architectural design I like:
Ideas from a co-worker or classmate I liked:	Notes:

Description:

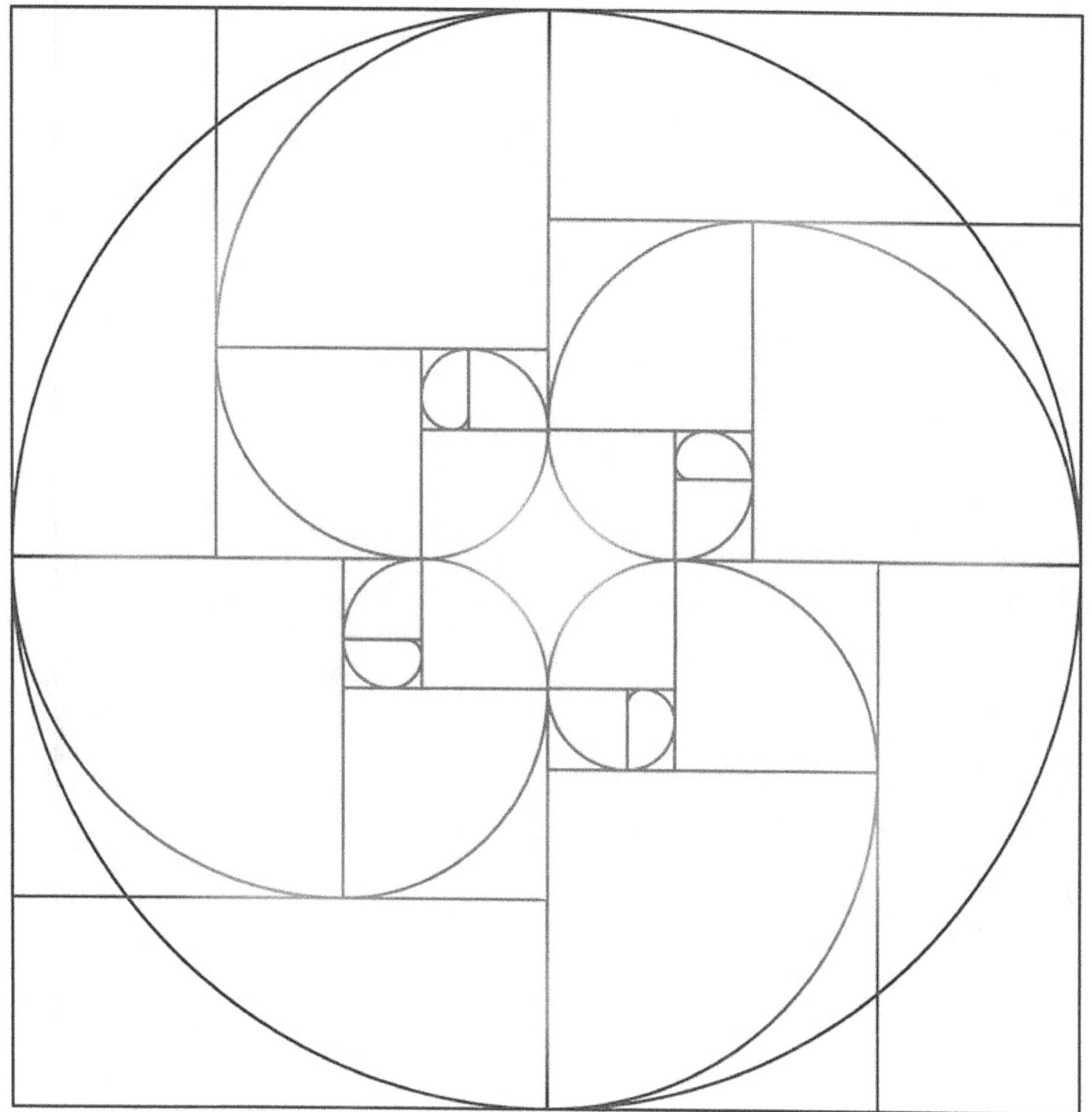

Date:		Day	

Websites to Note

Need to Purchase

Simple Day Planner

New Contacts-Friends

Books I Want to Remember

Music I Liked

TV/Movies I Liked

Project Updates

Five New Ideas

Social Media Links

Twitter	
Facebook	
Instagram	
Pinterest	
Snapchat	
Other	

Other Notes

Link to Page __________

Description:

Description:

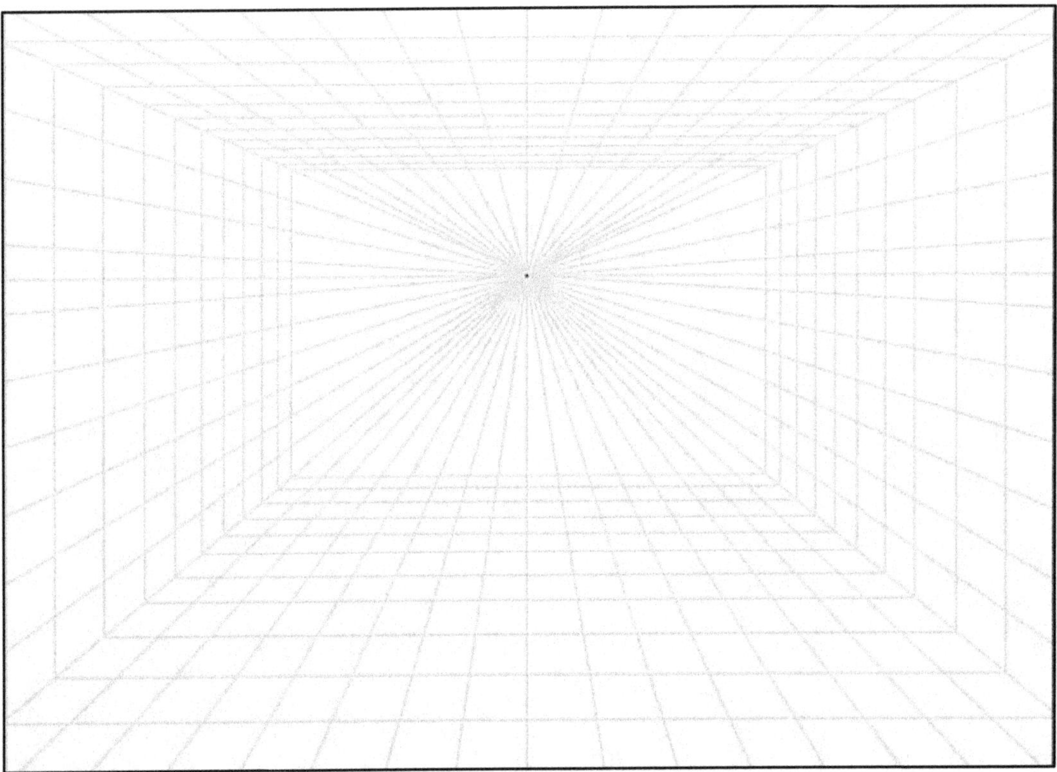

Description:

Description:

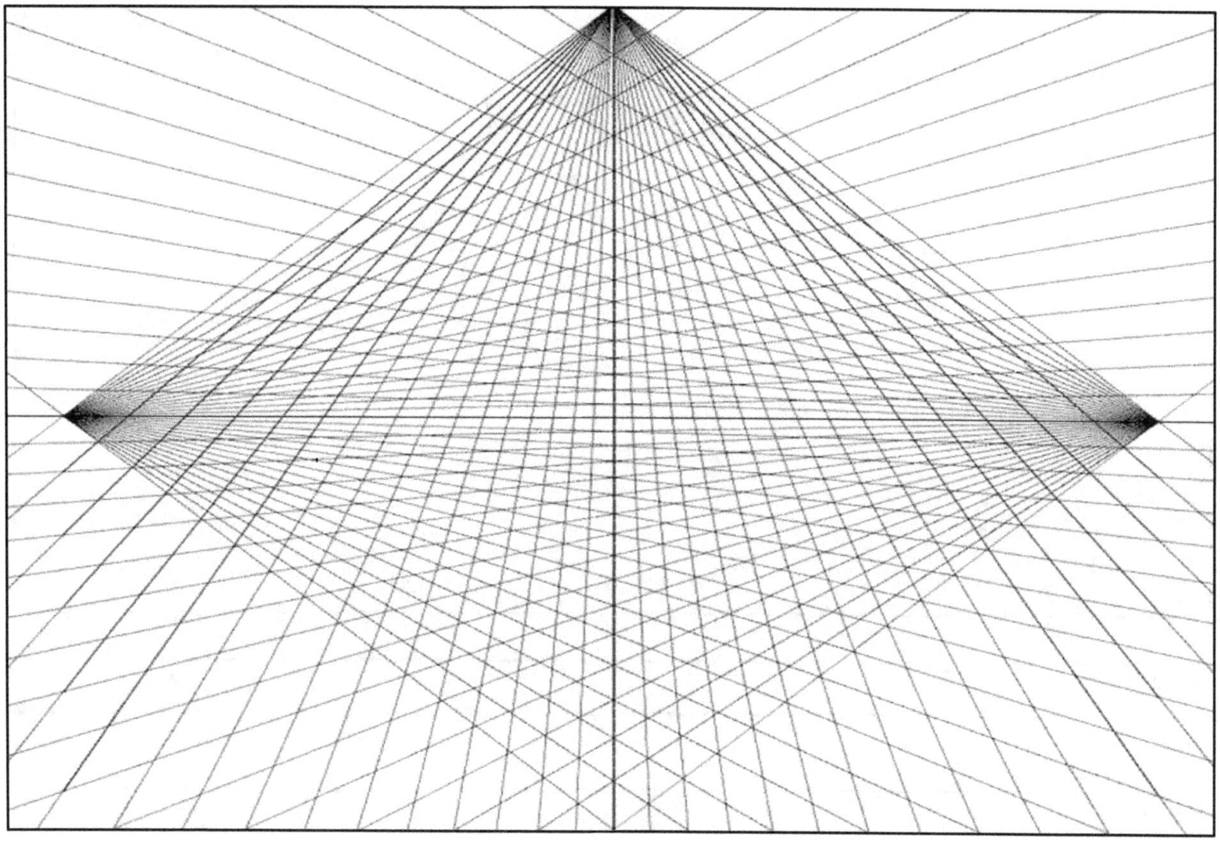

Description:

Description:

Description:

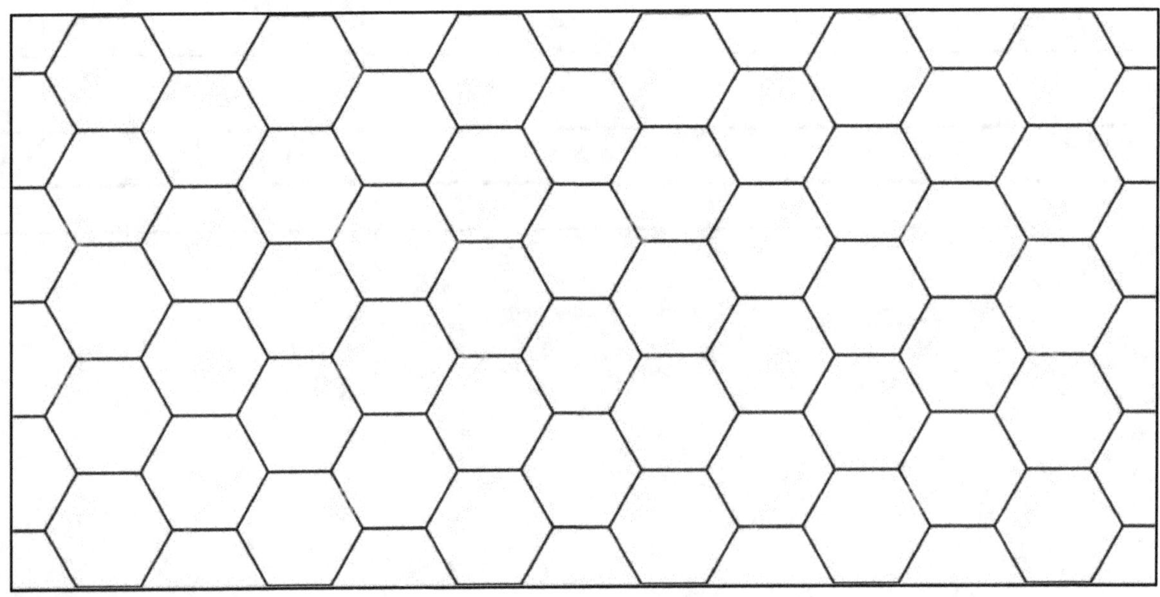

Description:

Description:

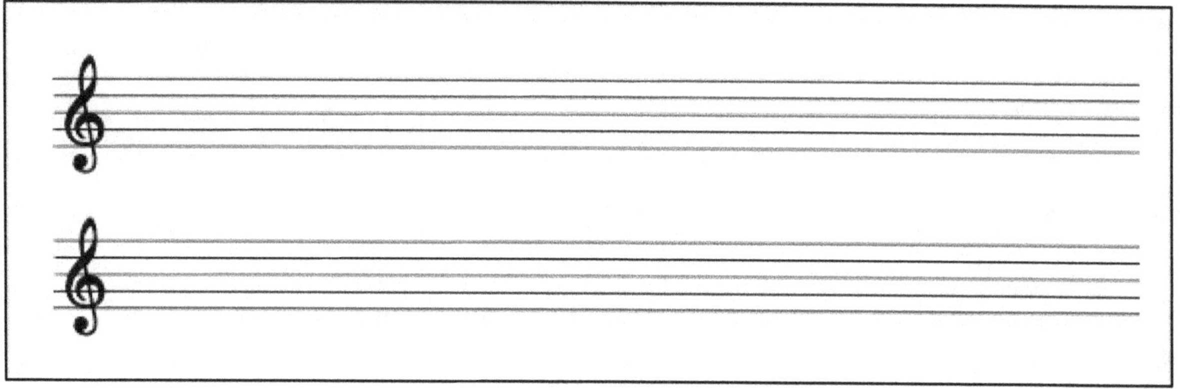

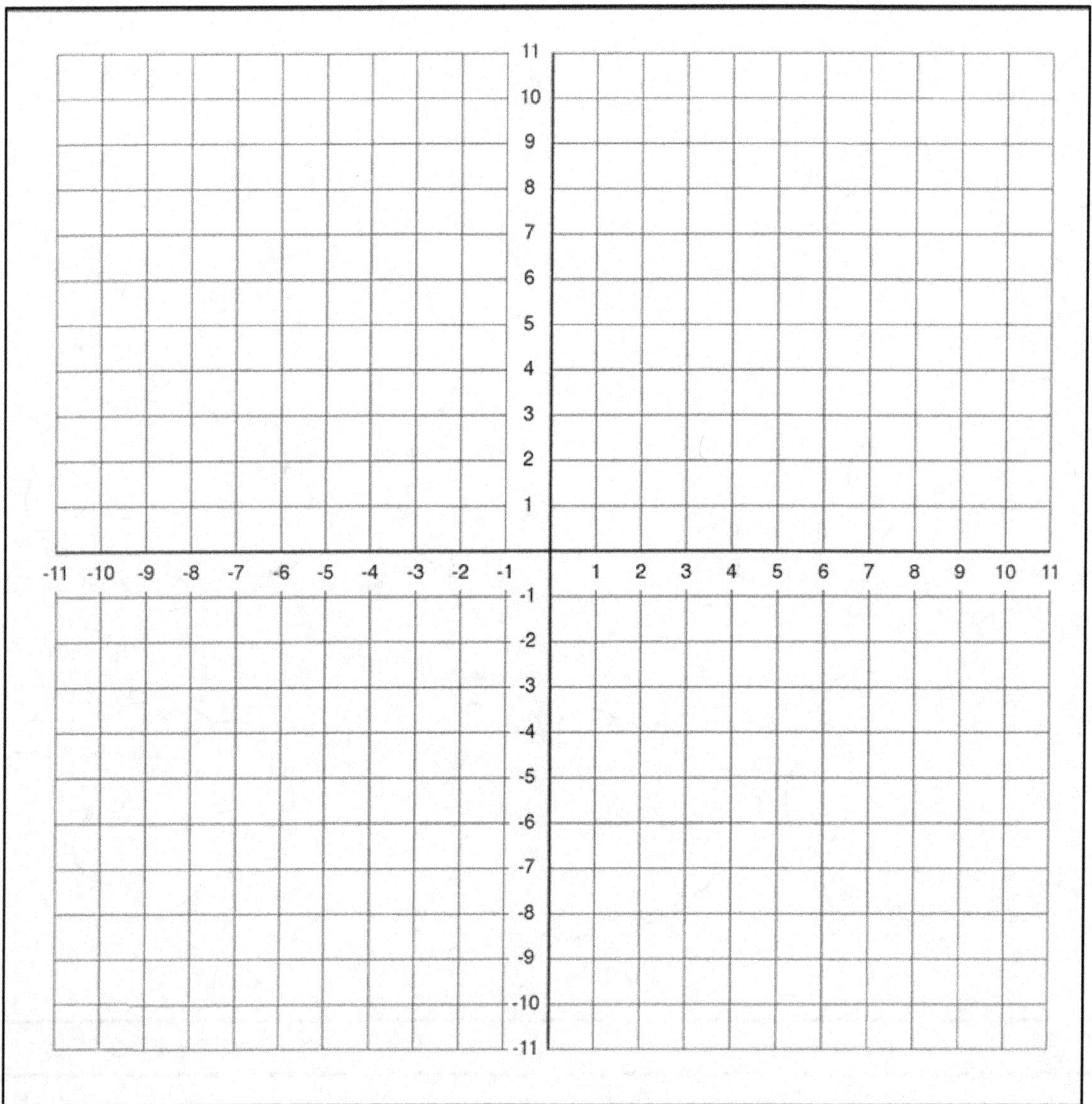

New words or phrases learned today:	Building or architectural design I like:
Ideas from a co-worker or classmate I liked:	Notes:

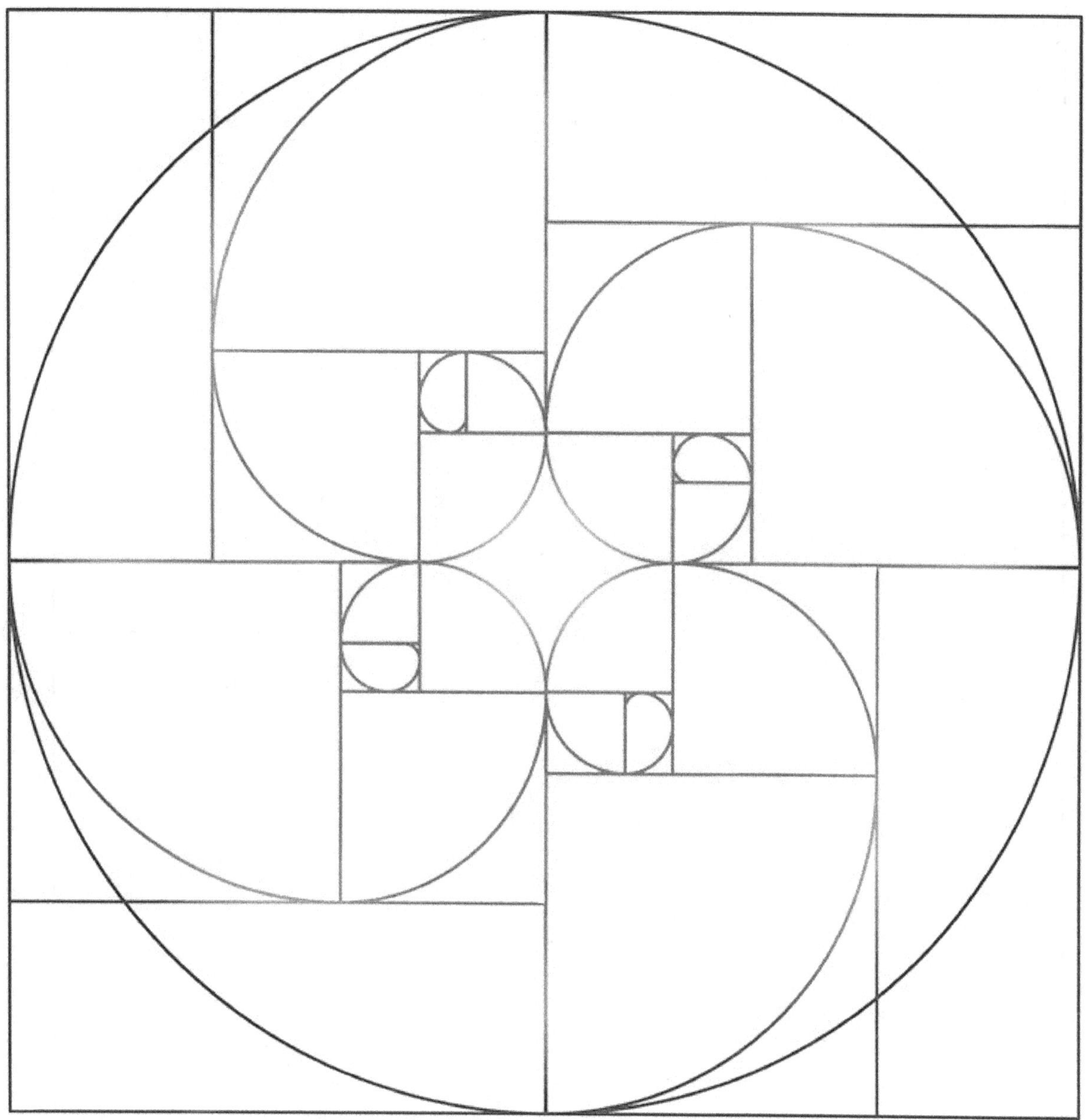

Description:

Date: | Day

Websites to Note

Simple Day Planner

Need to Purchase

New Contacts-Friends

Books I Want to Remember

Music I Liked

TV/Movies I Liked

Project Updates

Five New Ideas

Social Media Links

Twitter	
Facebook	
Instagram	
Pinterest	
Snapchat	
Other	

Other Notes

Link to Page _________

Description:

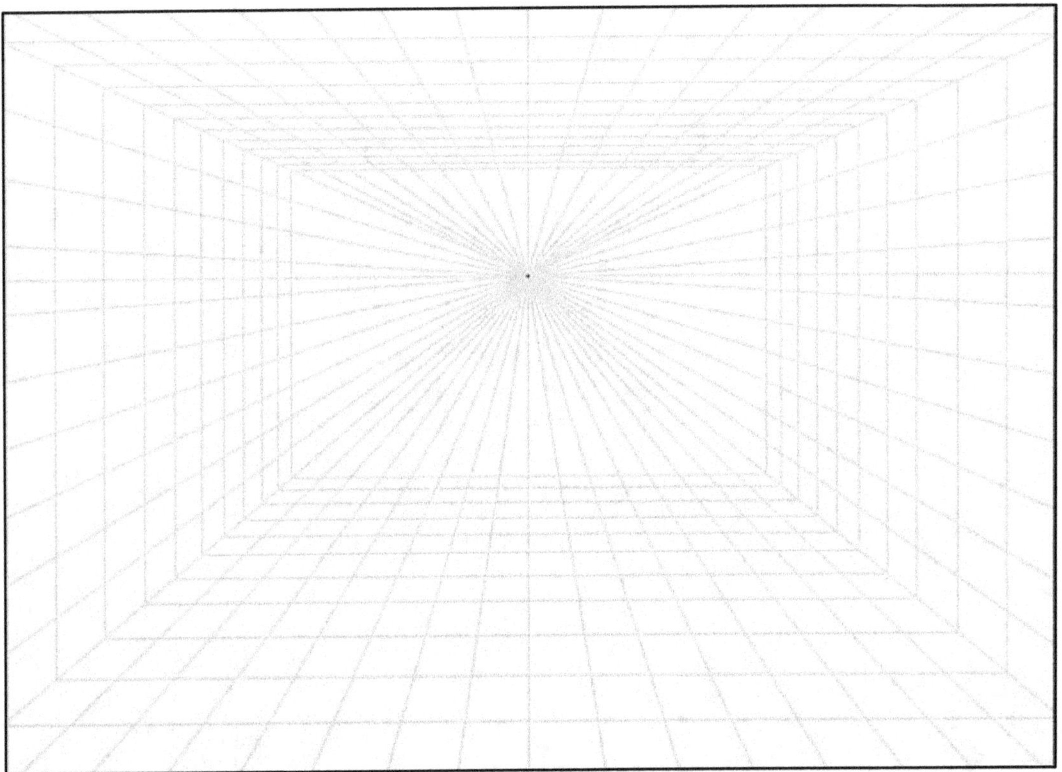

Description:

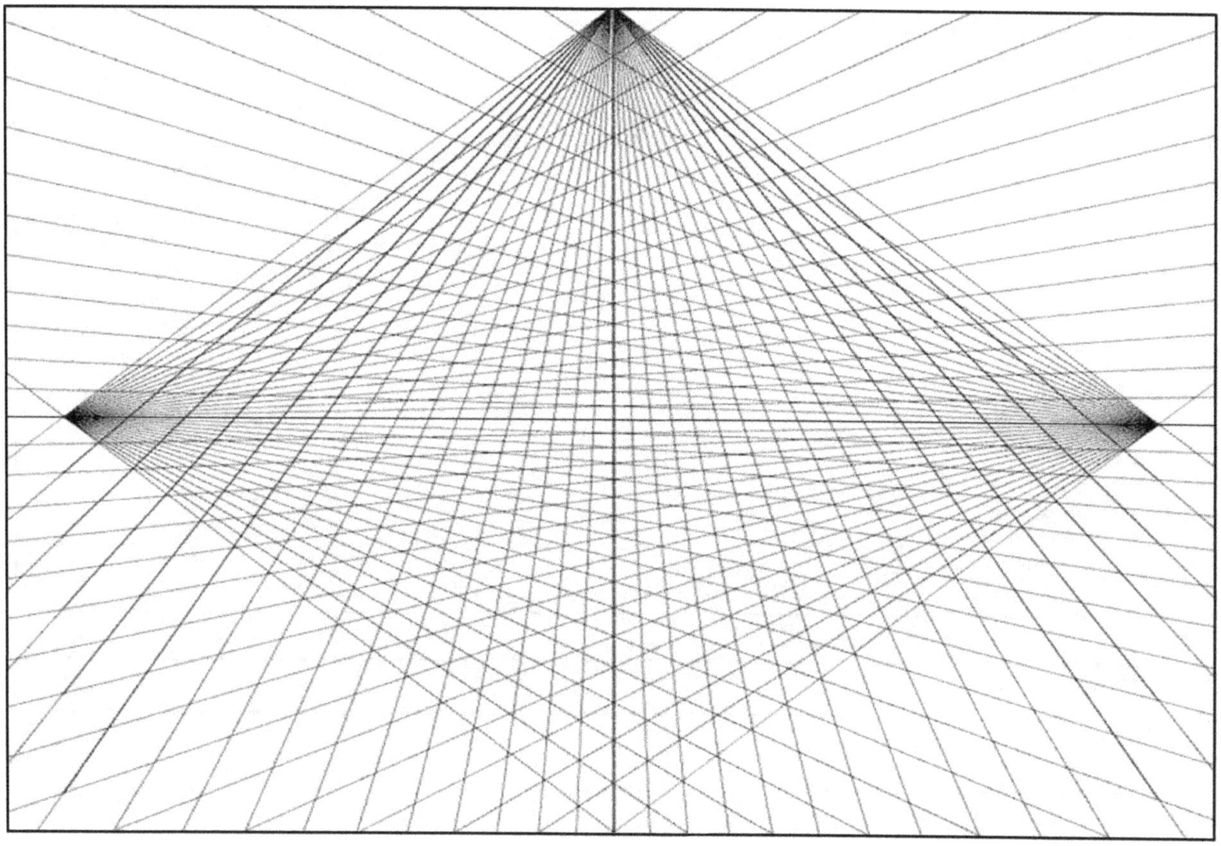

Description:

Description:

Description:

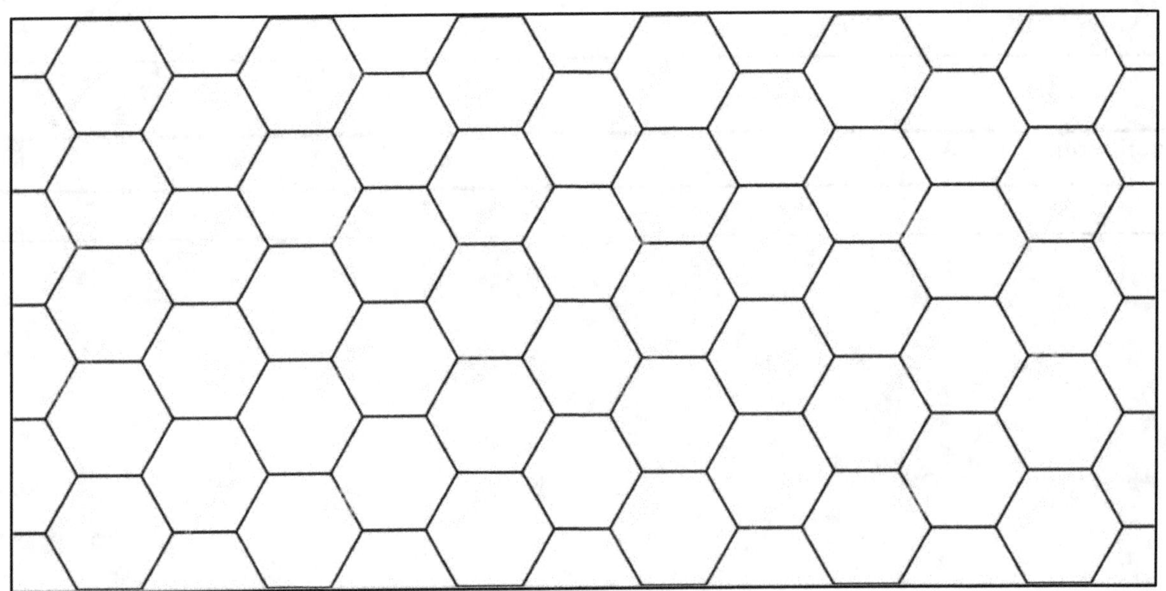

Description:

Description:

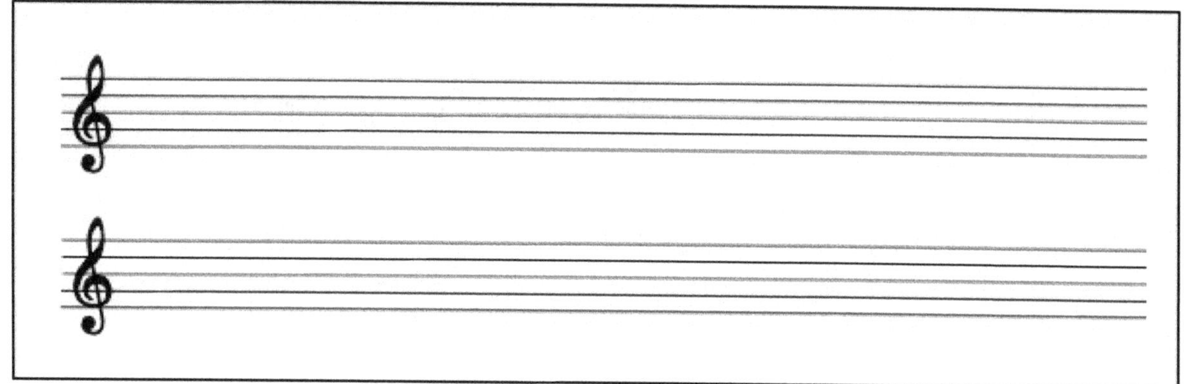

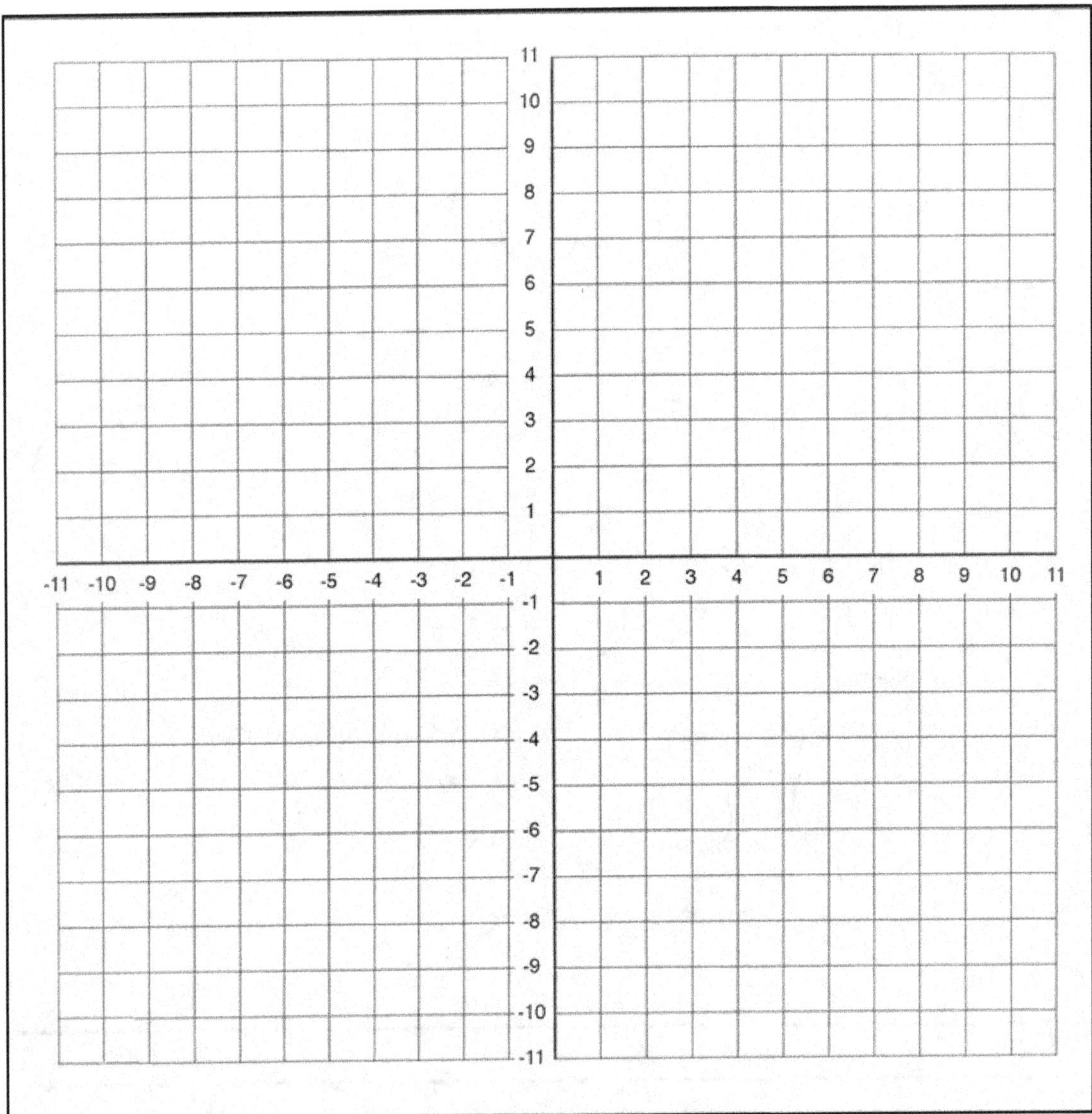

New words or phrases learned today:	Building or architectural design I like:
Ideas from a co-worker or classmate I liked:	Notes:

Description:

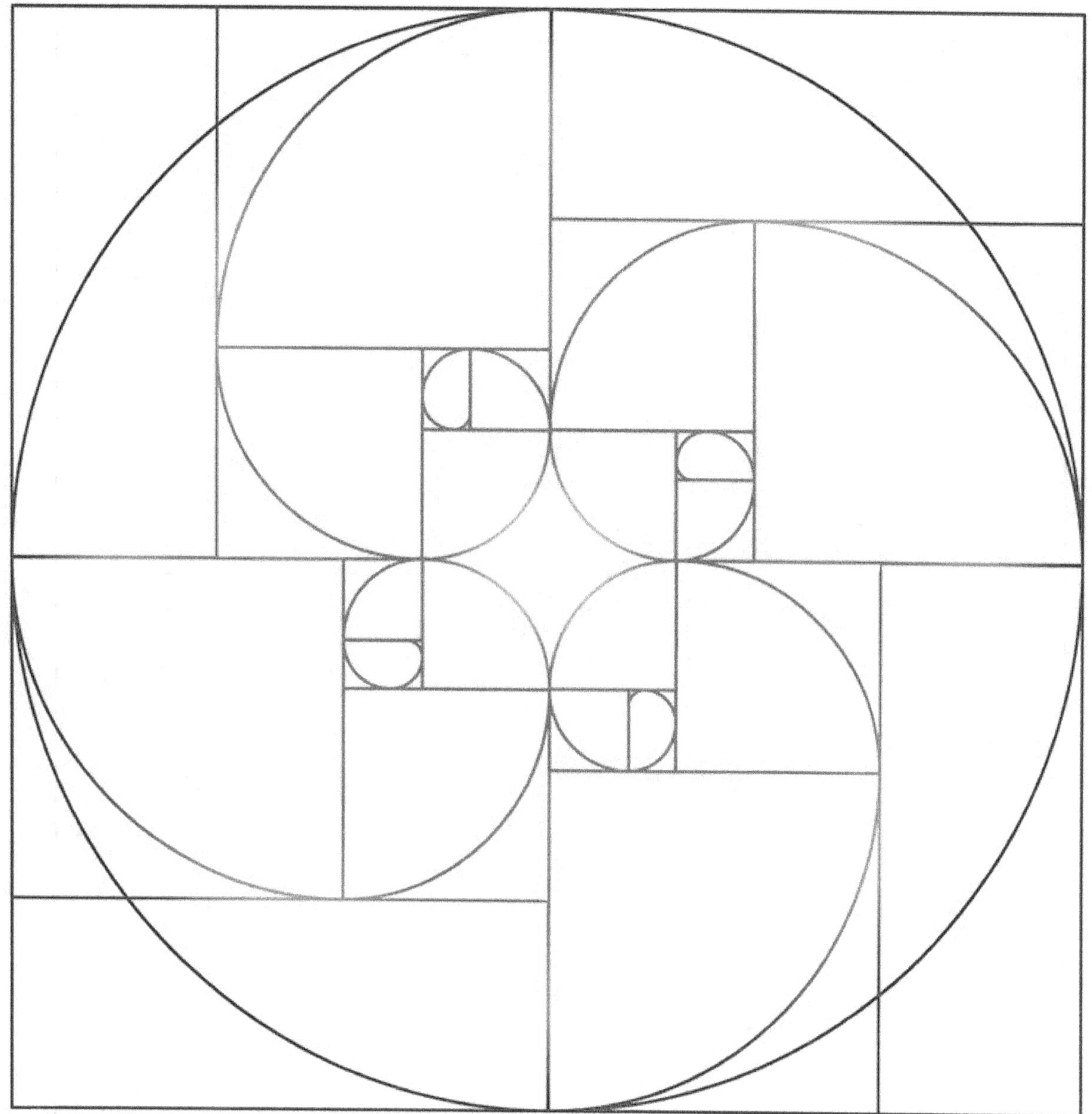

| Date: | | Day | |

Websites to Note

Need to Purchase

Simple Day Planner

New Contacts-Friends

Project Updates

Books I Want to Remember

Music I Liked

TV/Movies I Liked

Five New Ideas

Social Media Links

Twitter	
Facebook	
Instagram	
Pinterest	
Snapchat	
Other	

Other Notes

Link to Page __________

Description:

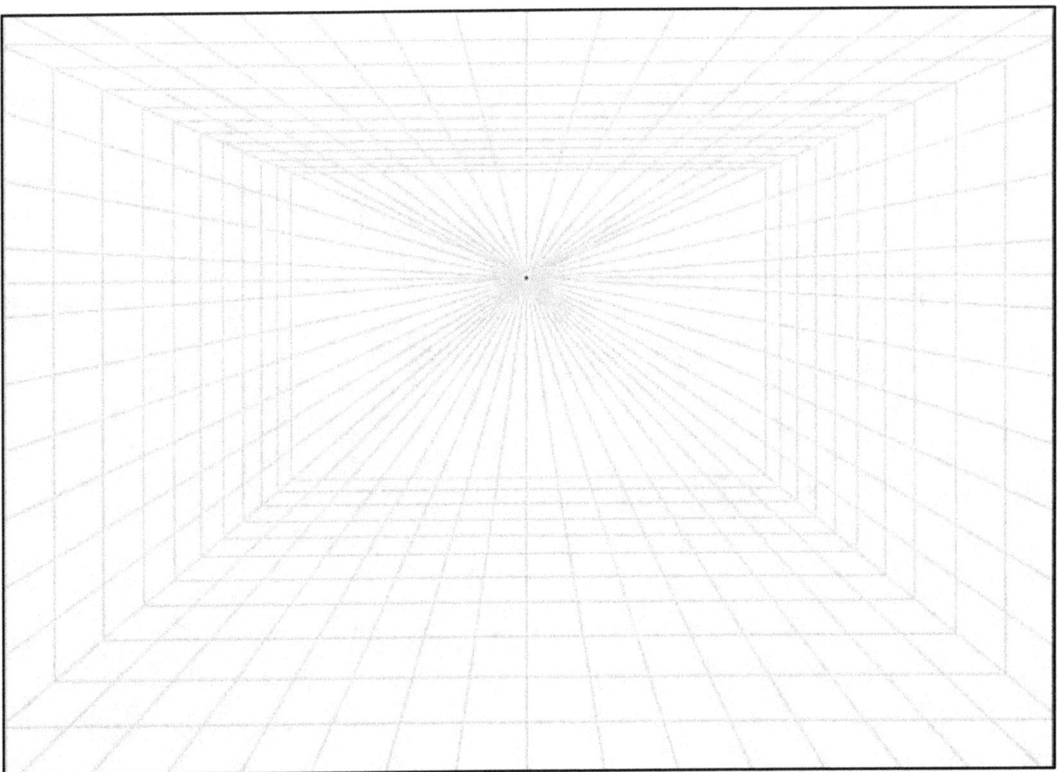

Description:

Description:

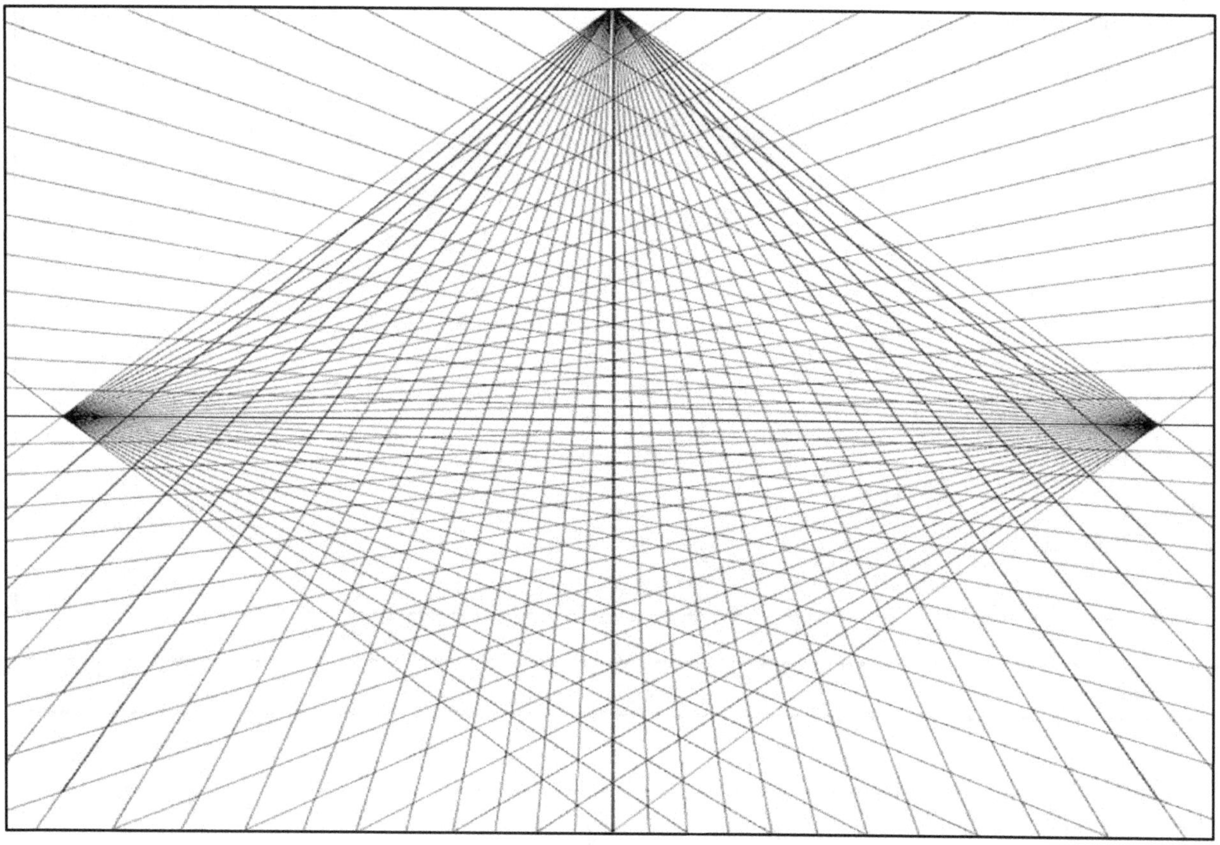

Description:

Description:

Description:

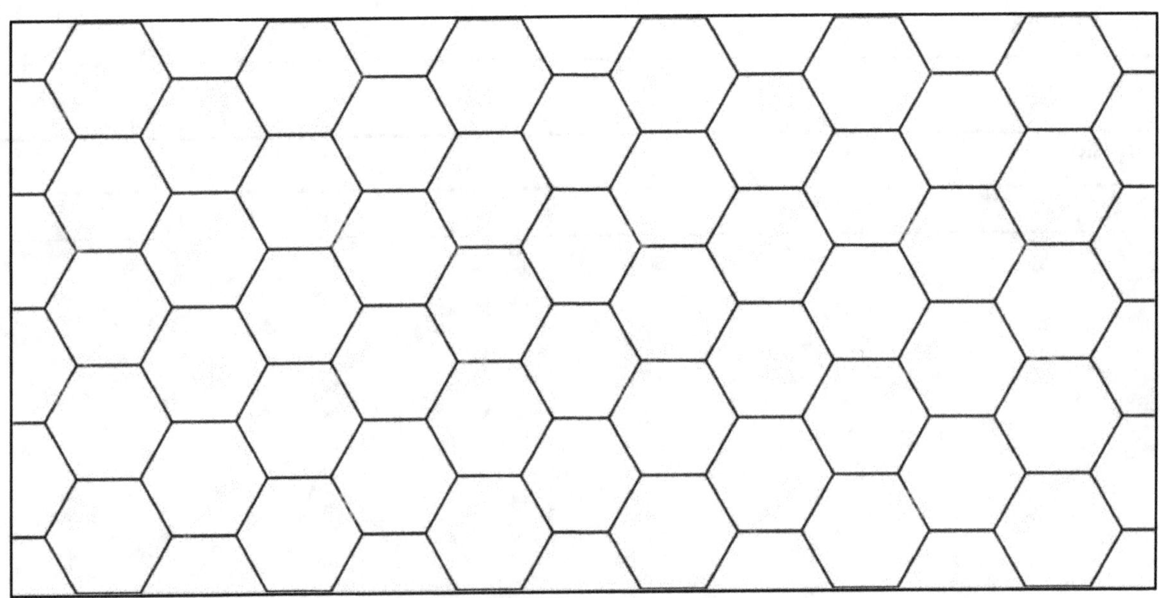

Description:

Description:

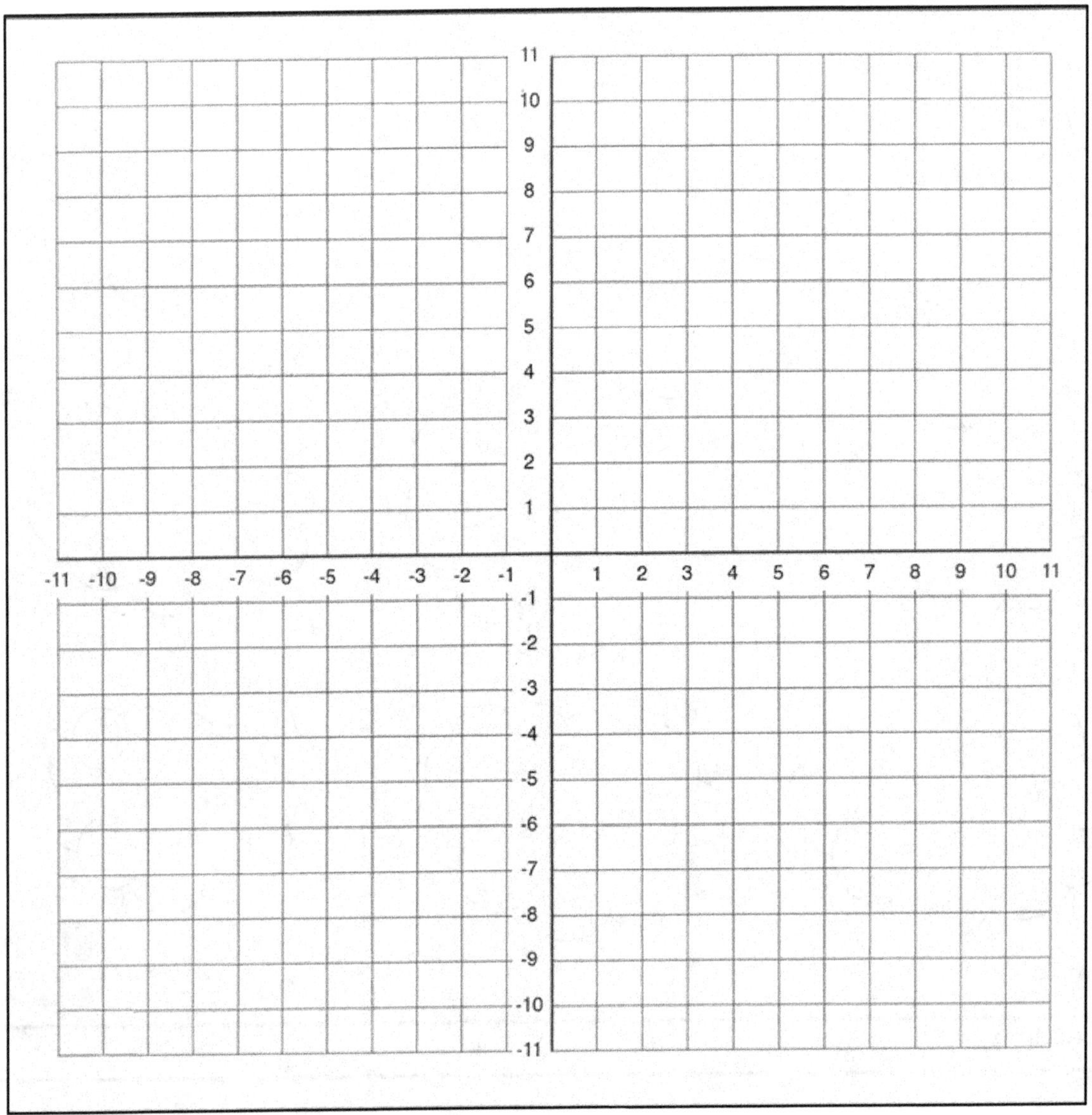

New words or phrases learned today:	Building or architectural design I like:
Ideas from a co-worker or classmate I liked:	Notes:

Description:

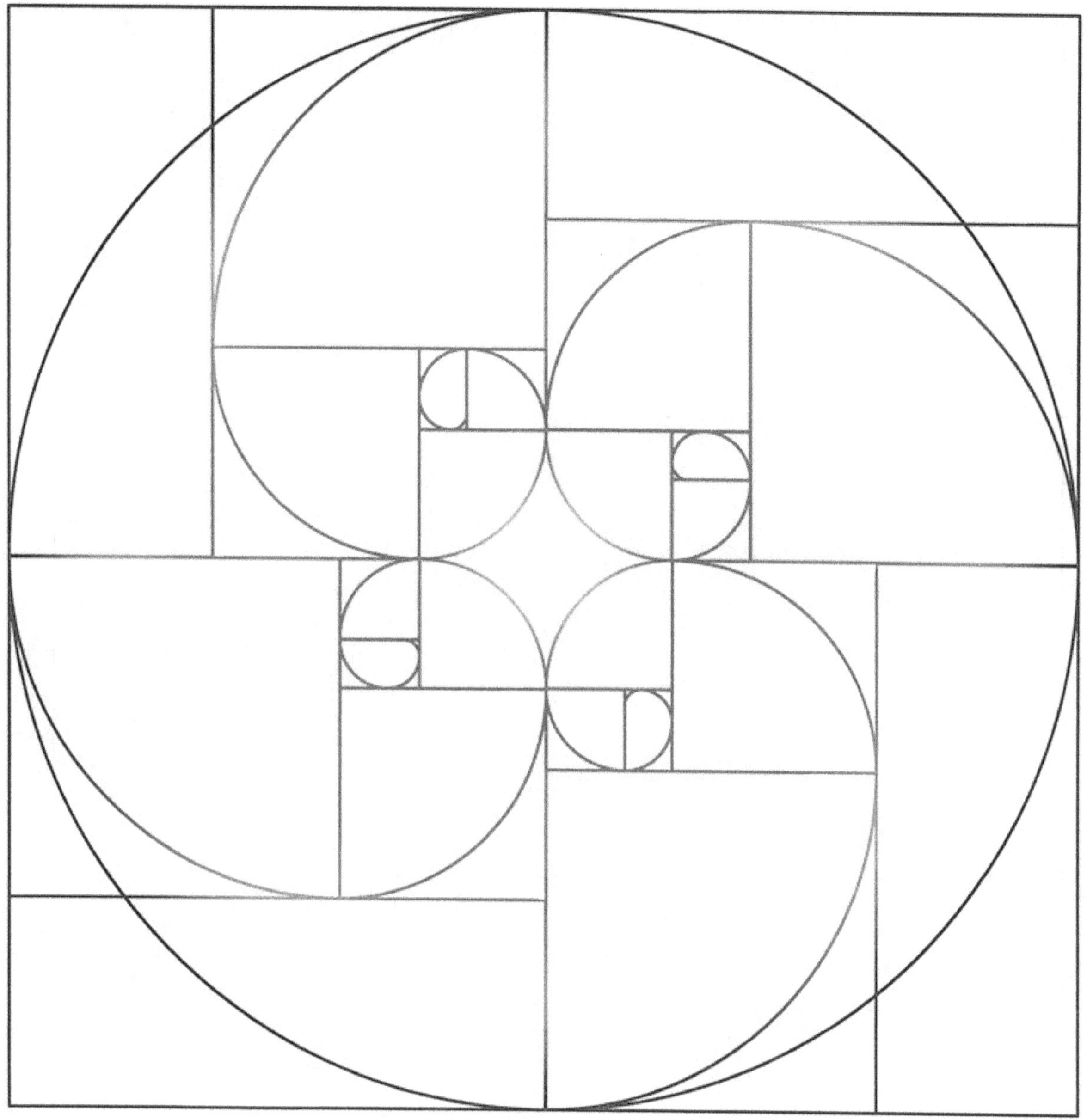

| Date: | | Day | |

Websites to Note

Need to Purchase

Simple Day Planner

New Contacts-Friends

Project Updates

Books I Want to Remember

Music I Liked

TV/Movies I Liked

Five New Ideas

Social Media Links

Twitter	
Facebook	
Instagram	
Pinterest	
Snapchat	
Other	

Other Notes

Link to Page __________

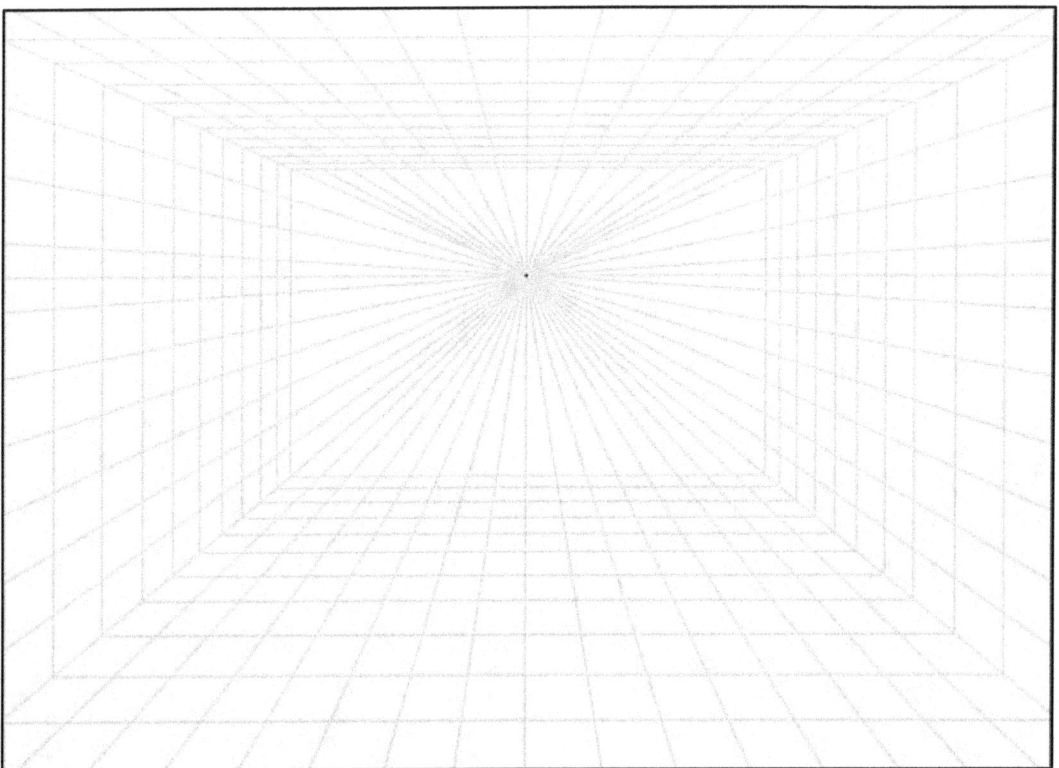

Description:

Description:

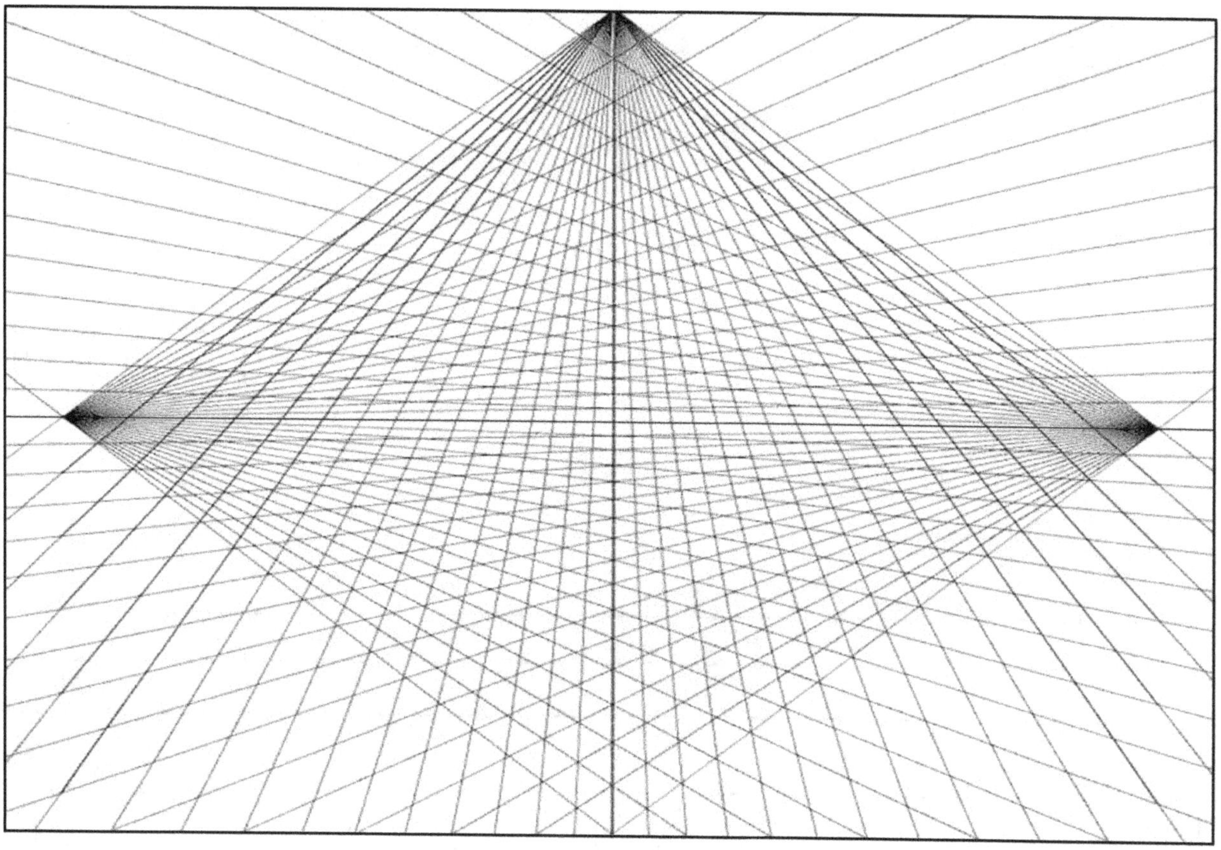

Description:

Description:

Description:

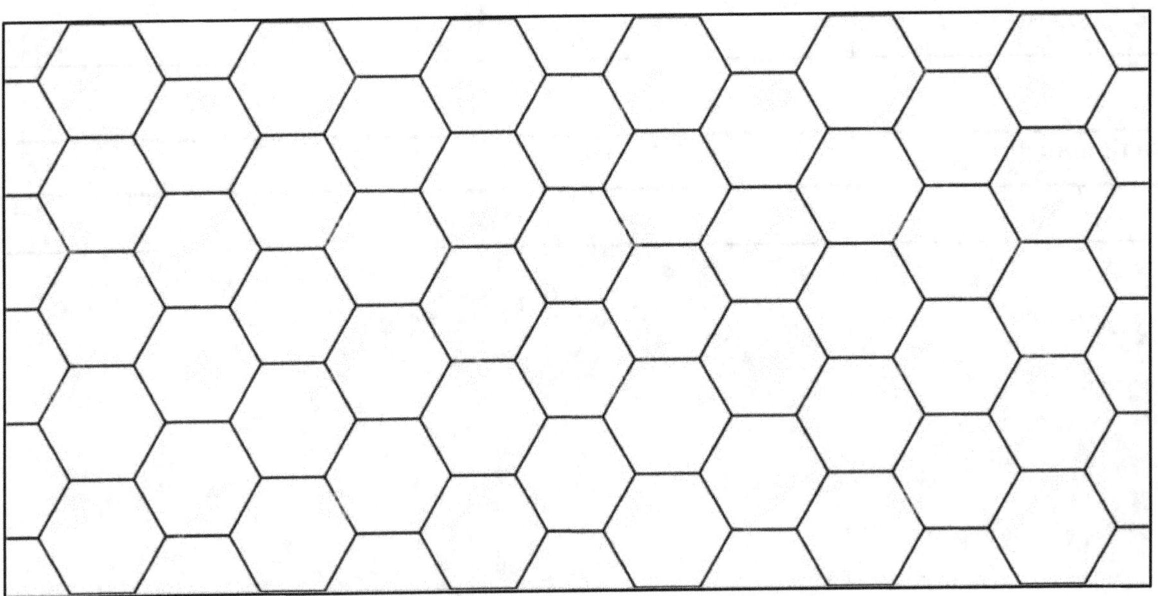

Description:

Description:

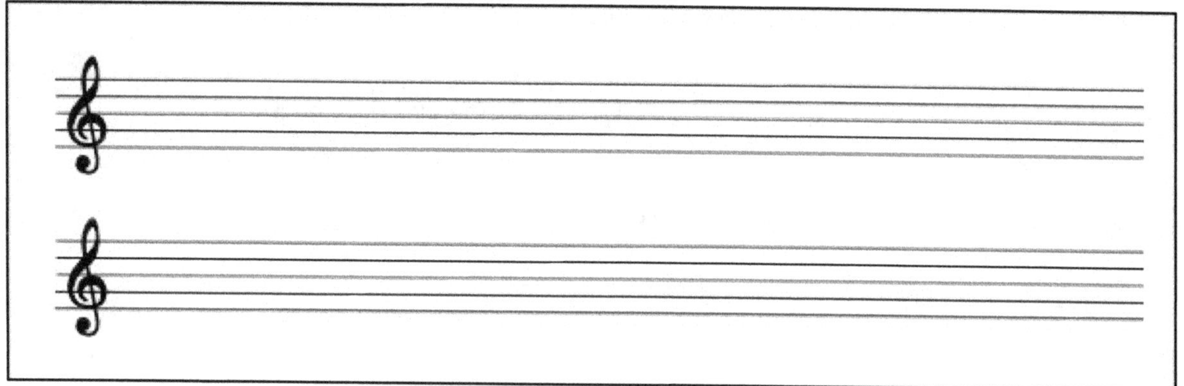

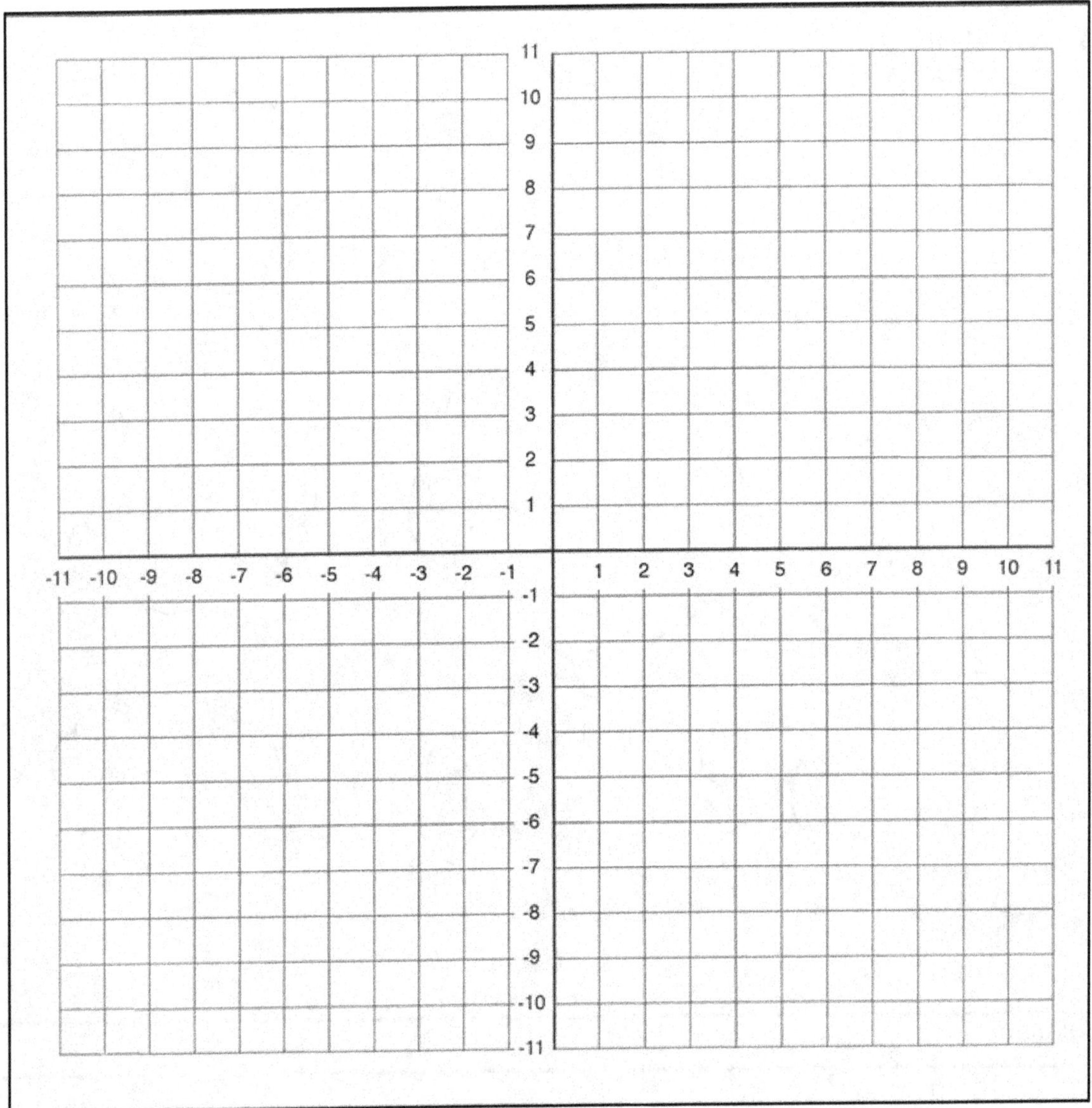

New words or phrases learned today:	Building or architectural design I like:
Ideas from a co-worker or classmate I liked:	Notes:

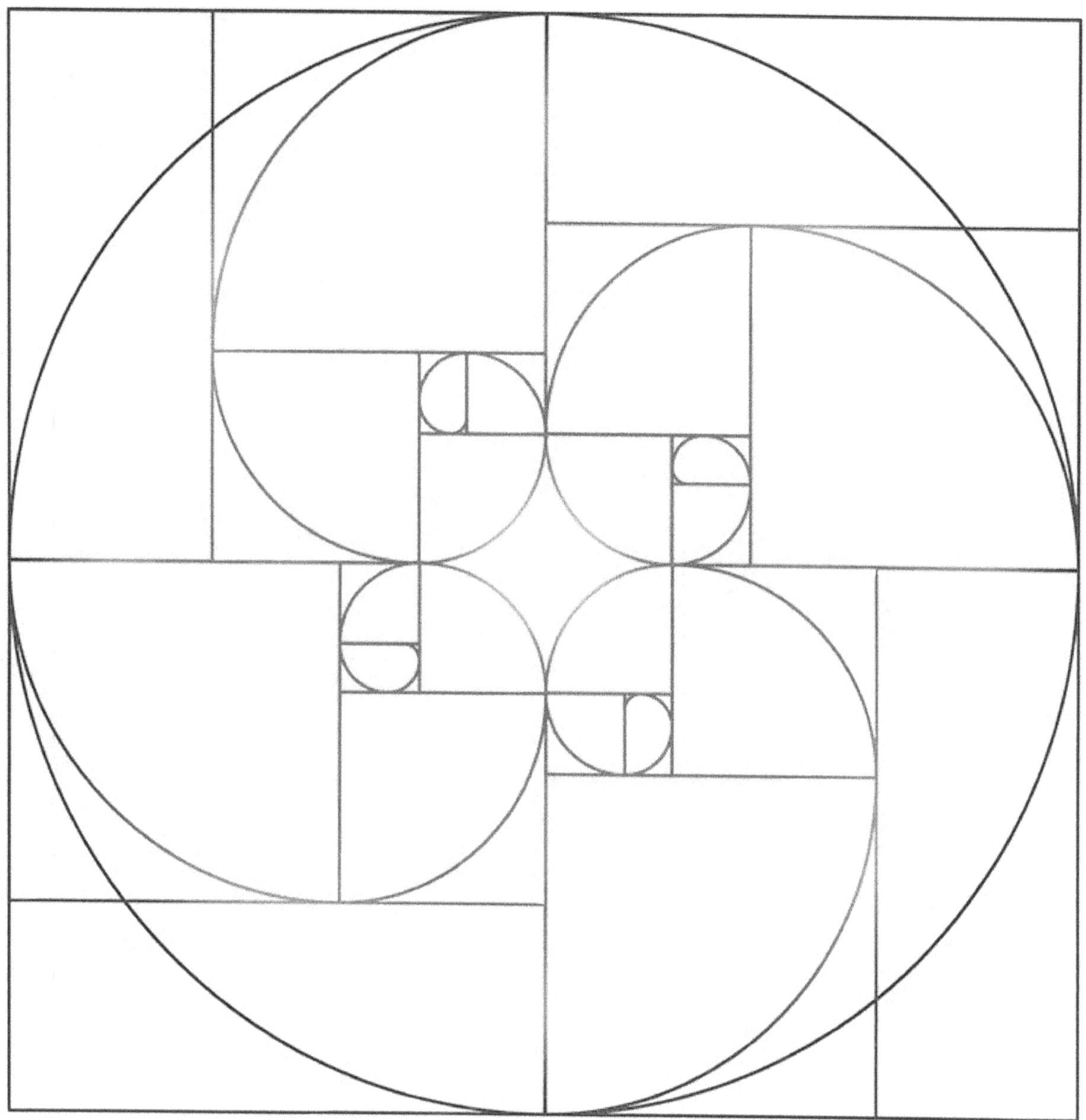

Date:		Day	

Websites to Note

Simple Day Planner

Need to Purchase

New Contacts-Friends

Books I Want to Remember

Music I Liked

Project Updates

TV/Movies I Liked

Five New Ideas

Social Media Links

Twitter	
Facebook	
Instagram	
Pinterest	
Snapchat	
Other	

Other Notes

Link to Page _________

Description:

Description:

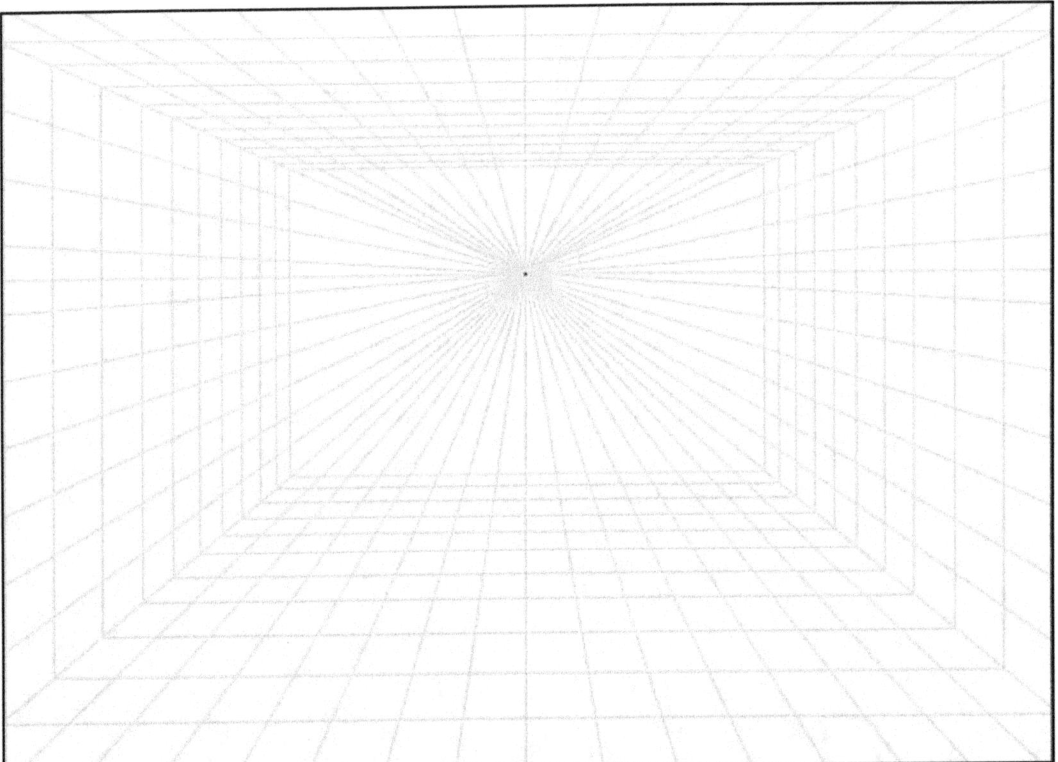

Description:

Description:

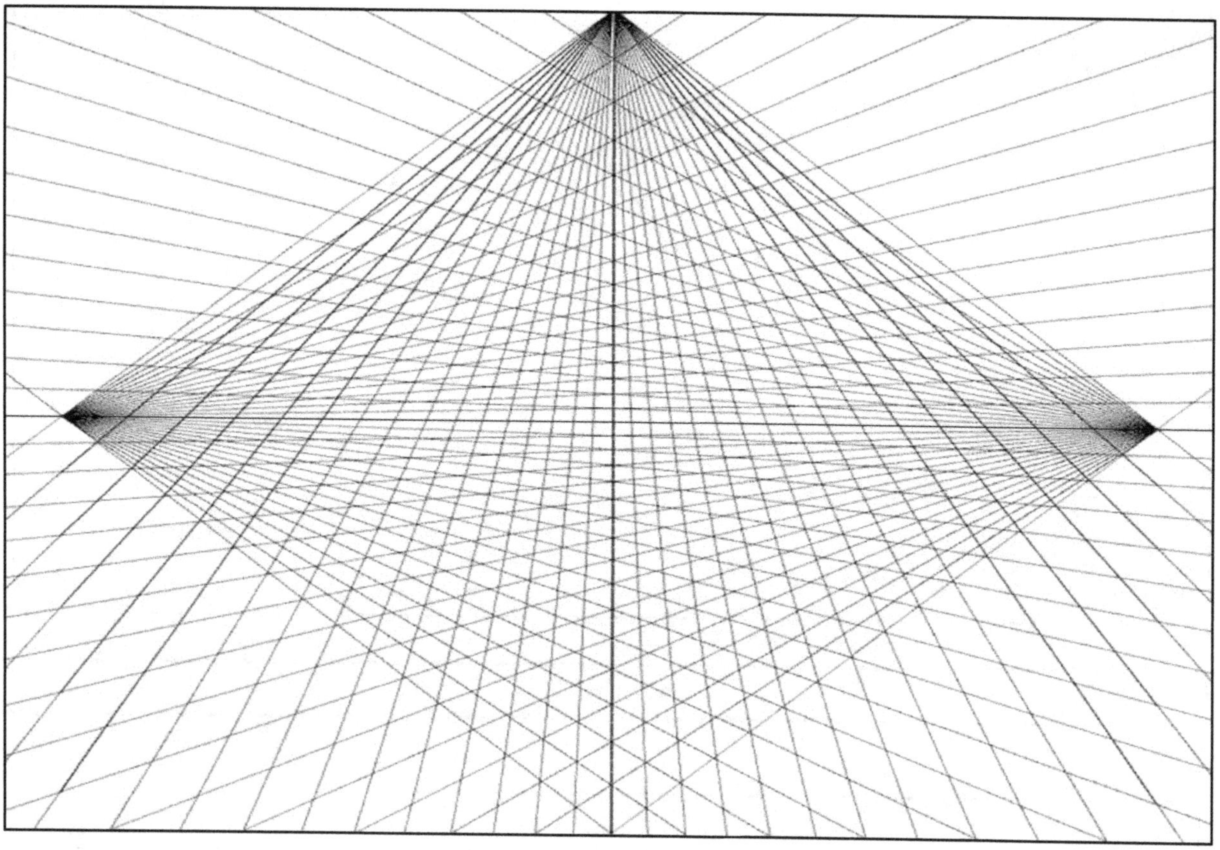

Description:

Description:

Description:

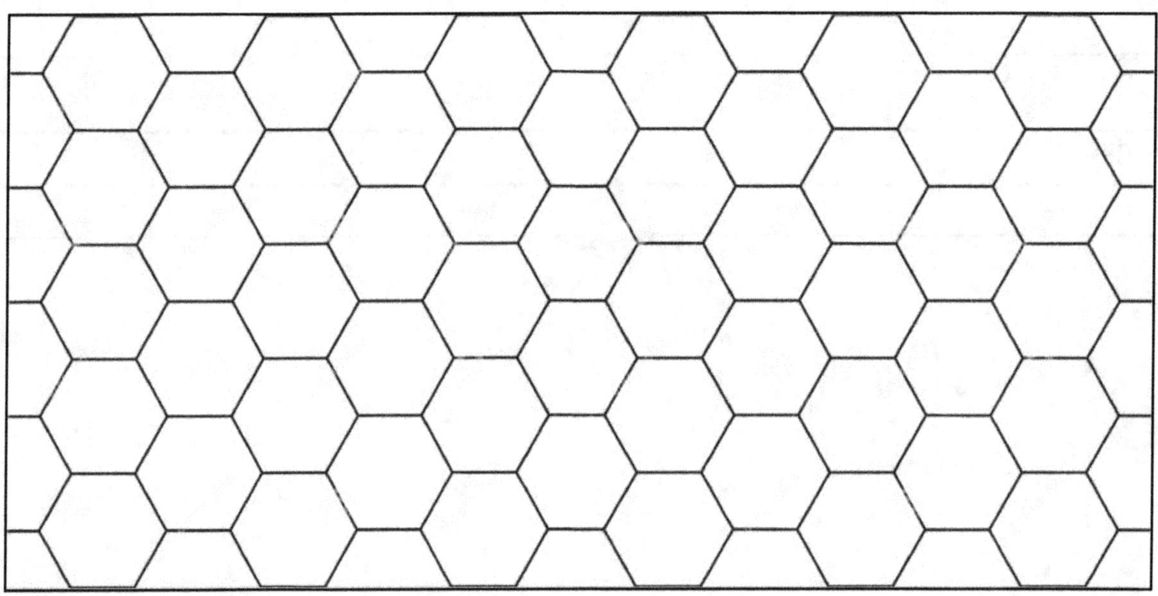

Description:

Description:

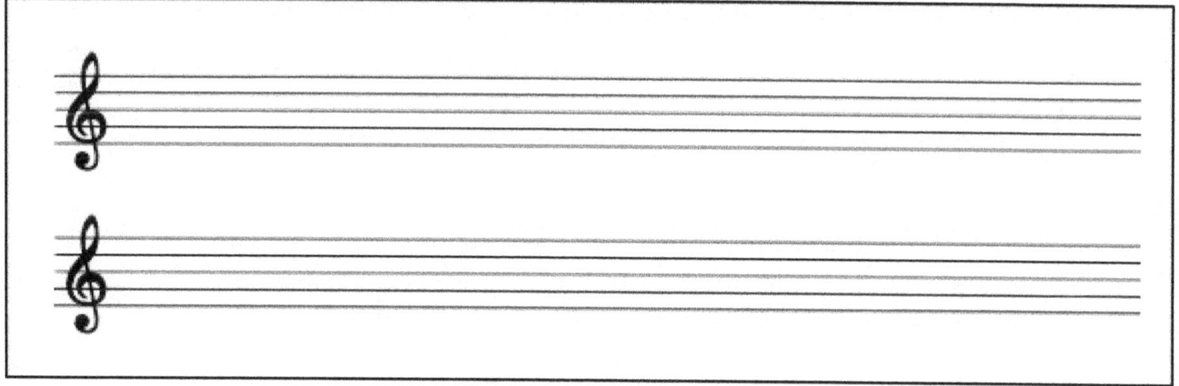

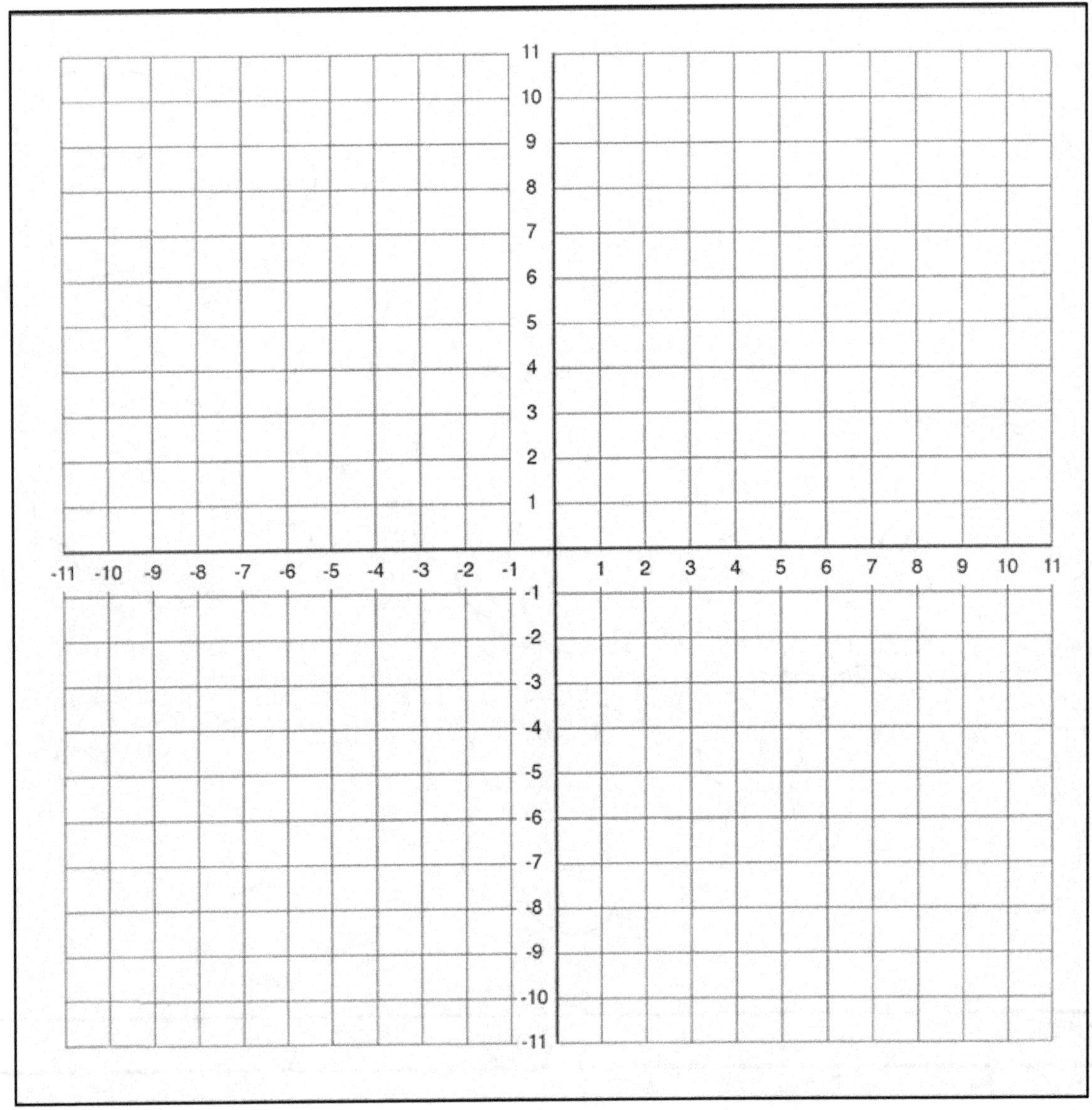

New words or phrases learned today:	Building or architectural design I like:
Ideas from a co-worker or classmate I liked:	Notes:

Description:

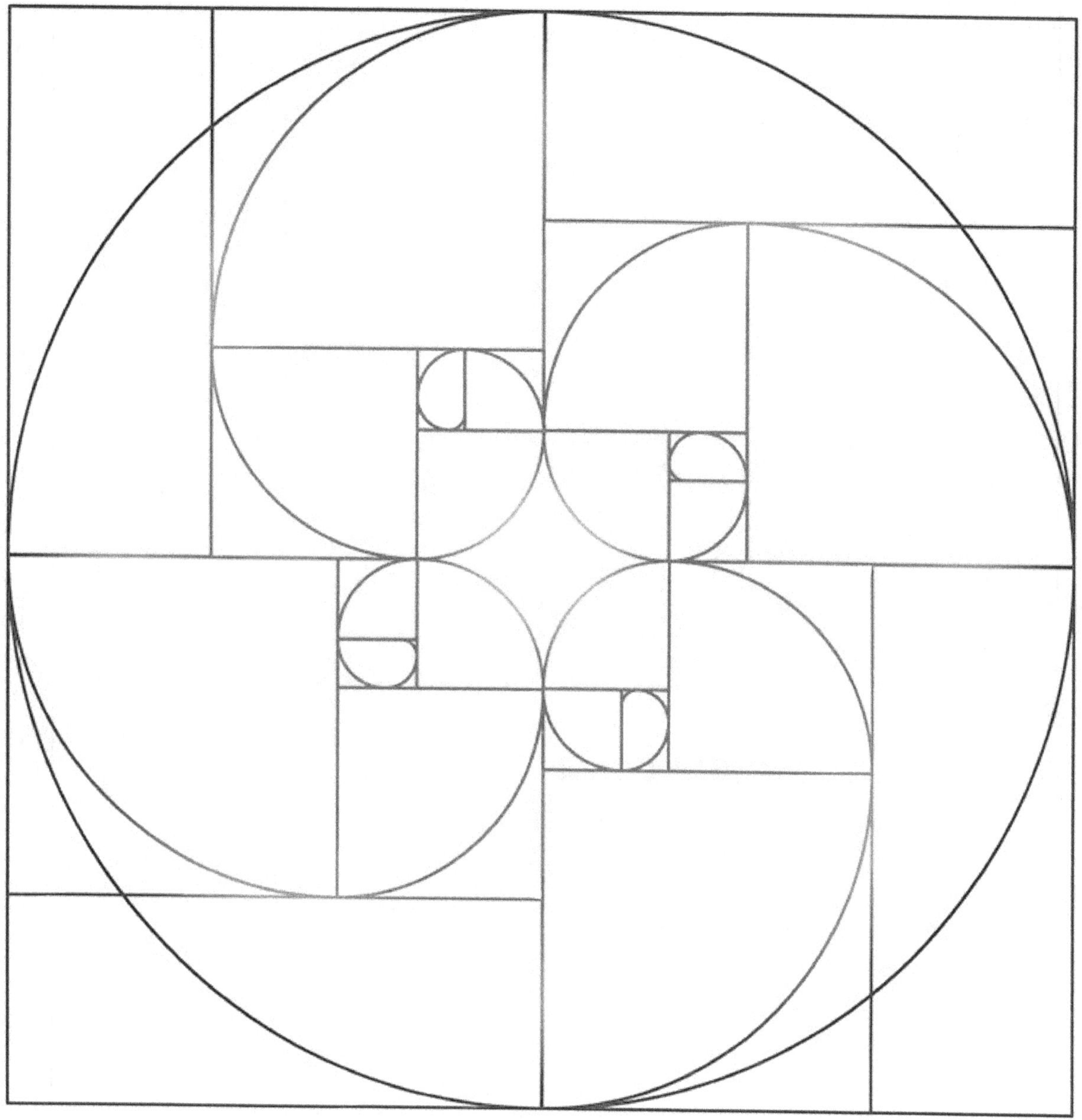

| Date: | | Day | |

Websites to Note

Need to Purchase

Simple Day Planner

New Contacts-Friends

Books I Want to Remember

Music I Liked

Project Updates

TV/Movies I Liked

Five New Ideas

Social Media Links

Twitter	
Facebook	
Instagram	
Pinterest	
Snapchat	
Other	

Other Notes

Link to Page __________

Description:

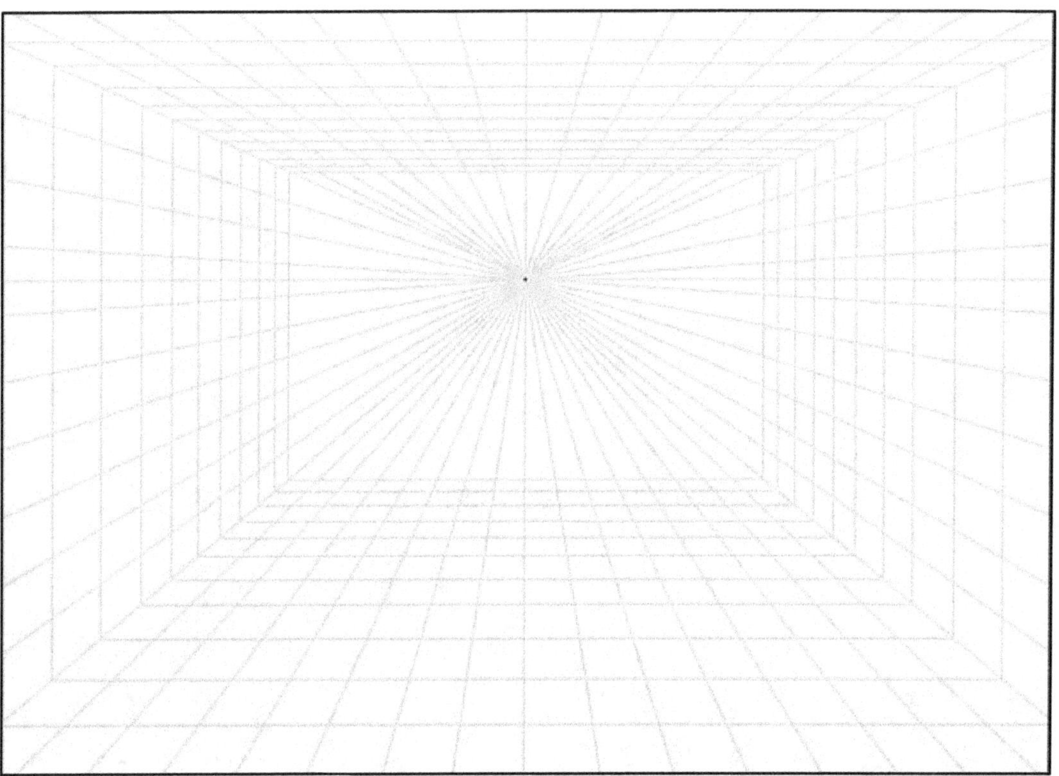

Description:

Description:

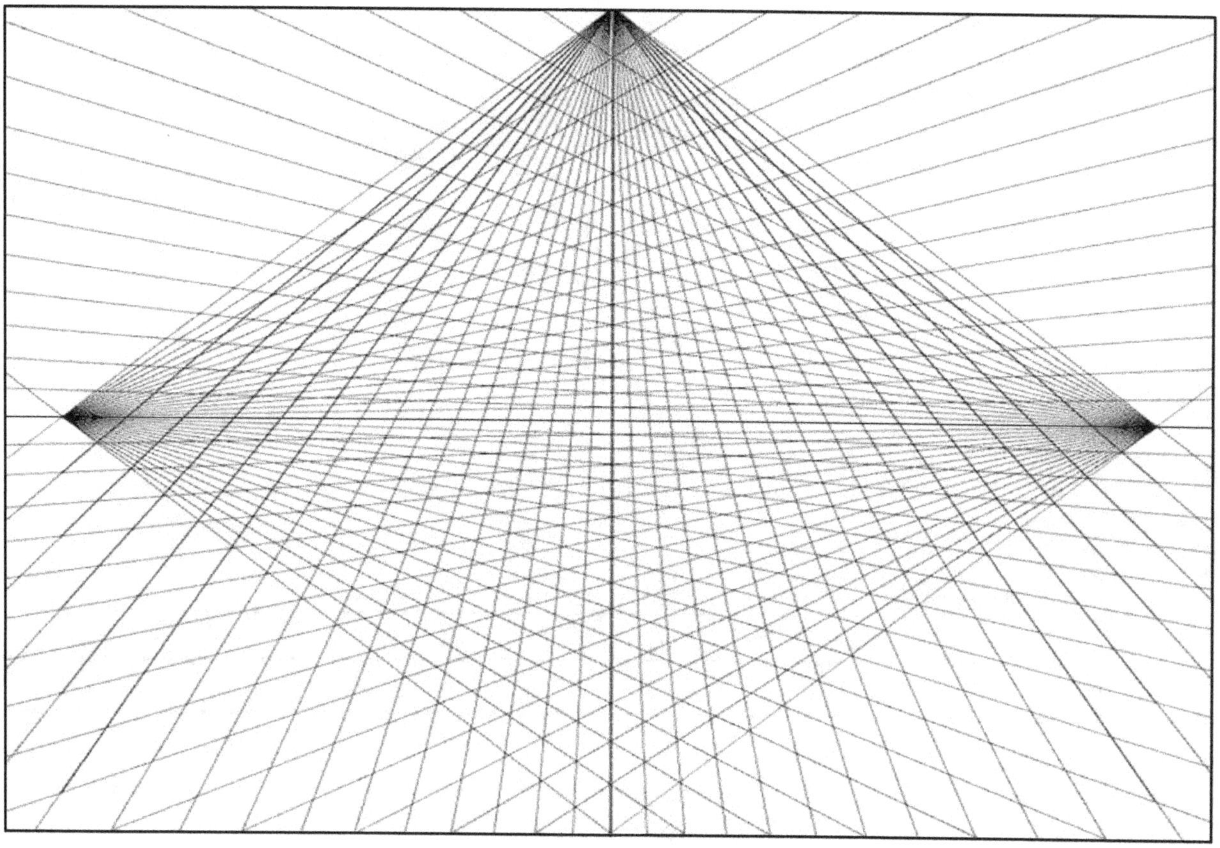

Description:

Description:

Description:

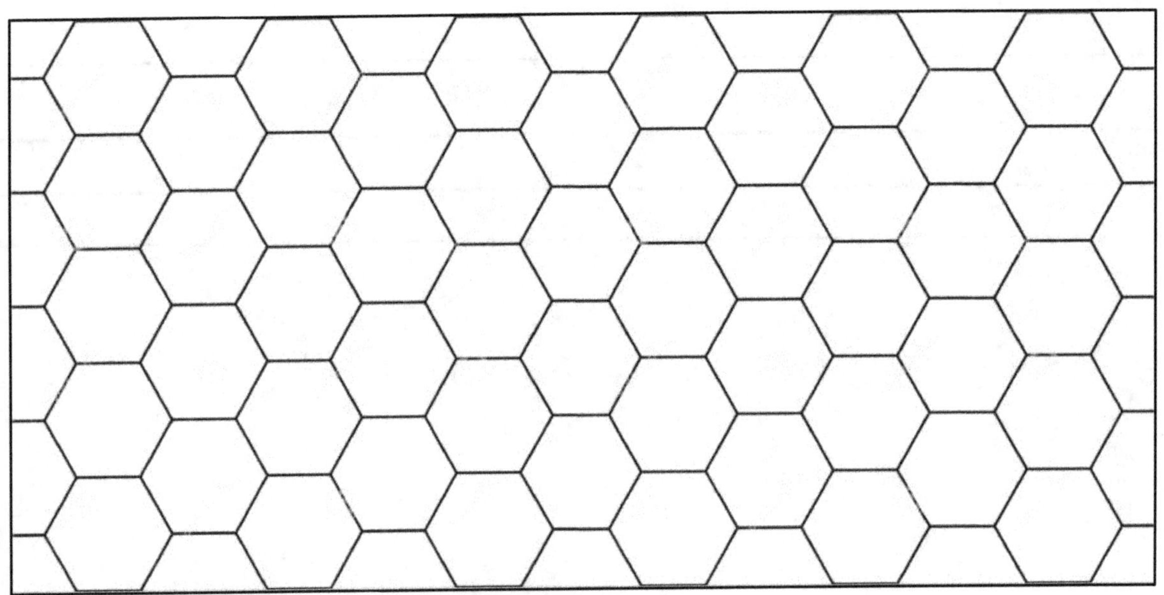

Description:

Description:

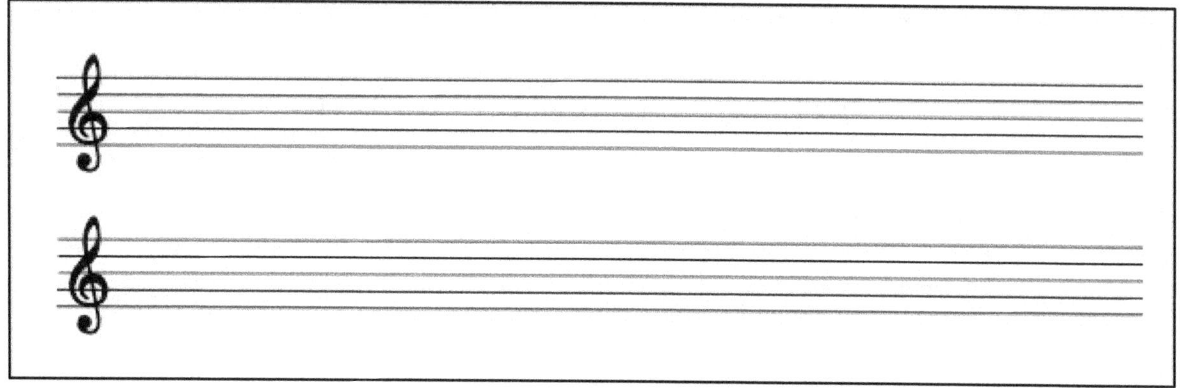

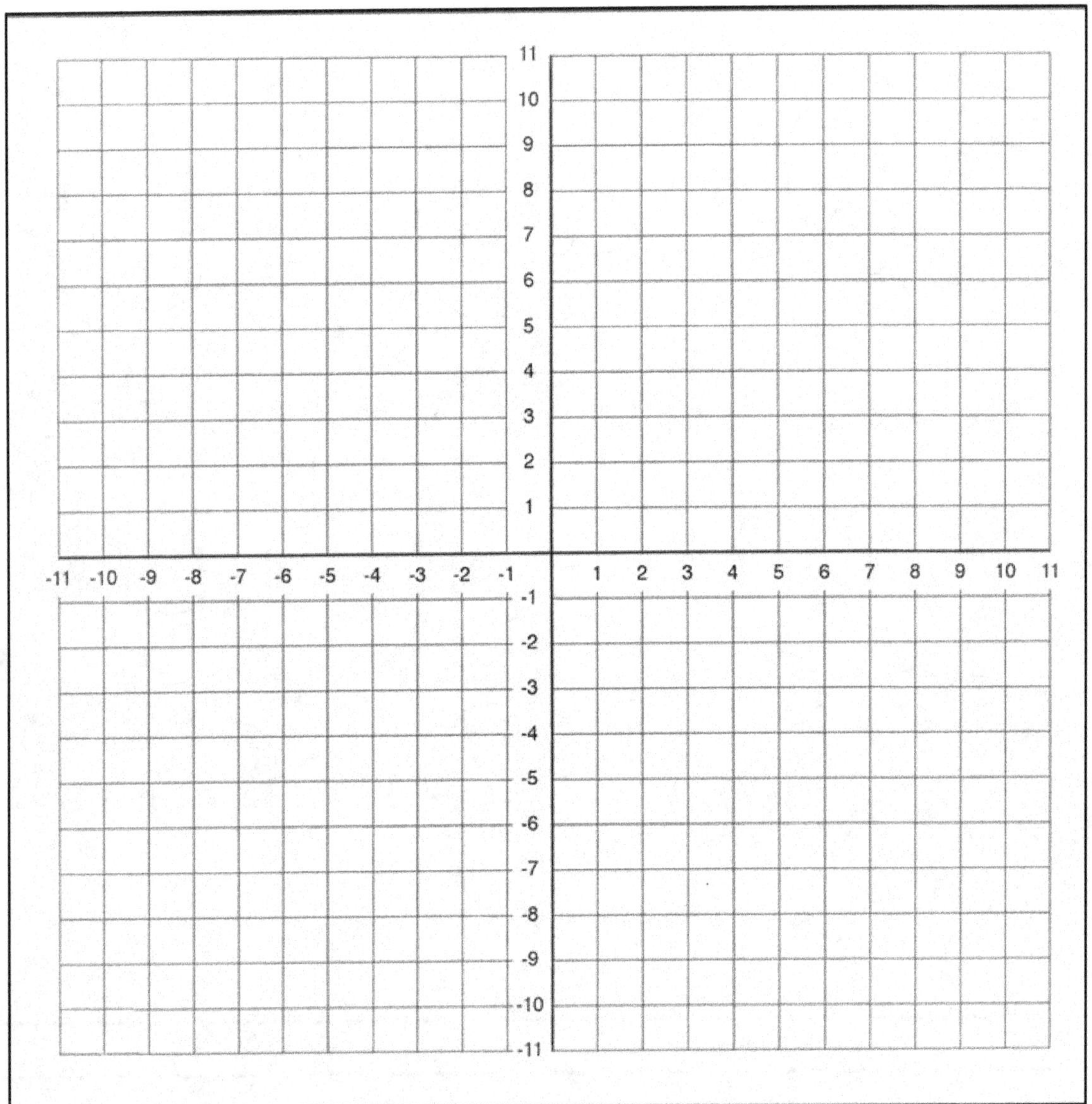

New words or phrases learned today:	Building or architectural design I like:
Ideas from a co-worker or classmate I liked:	Notes:

Description:

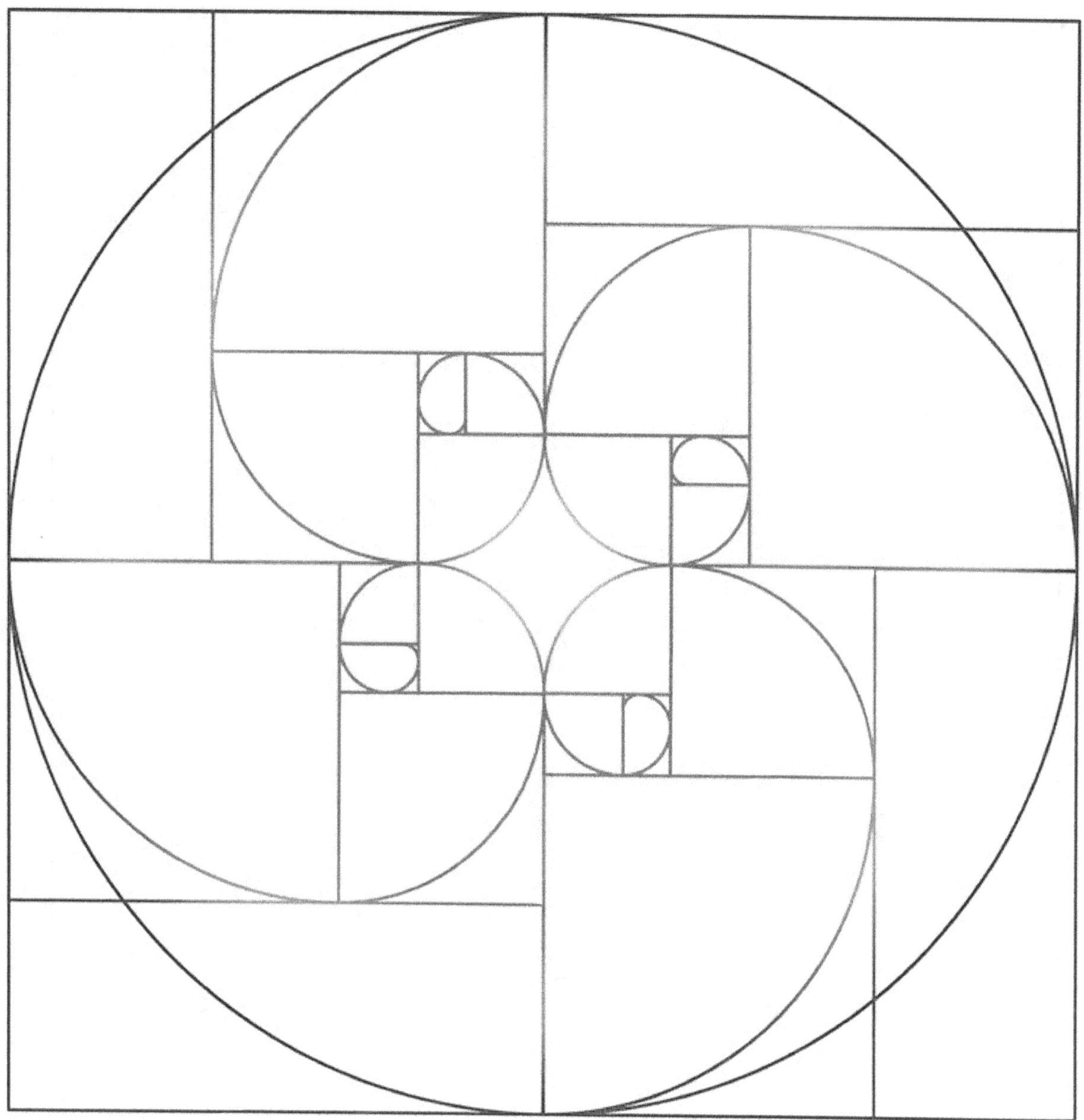

| Date: | | Day | |

Websites to Note

Simple Day Planner

Need to Purchase

New Contacts-Friends

Books I Want to Remember

Music I Liked

Project Updates

TV/Movies I Liked

Five New Ideas

Social Media Links

Twitter	
Facebook	
Instagram	
Pinterest	
Snapchat	
Other	

Other Notes

Link to Page _________

Description:

Description:

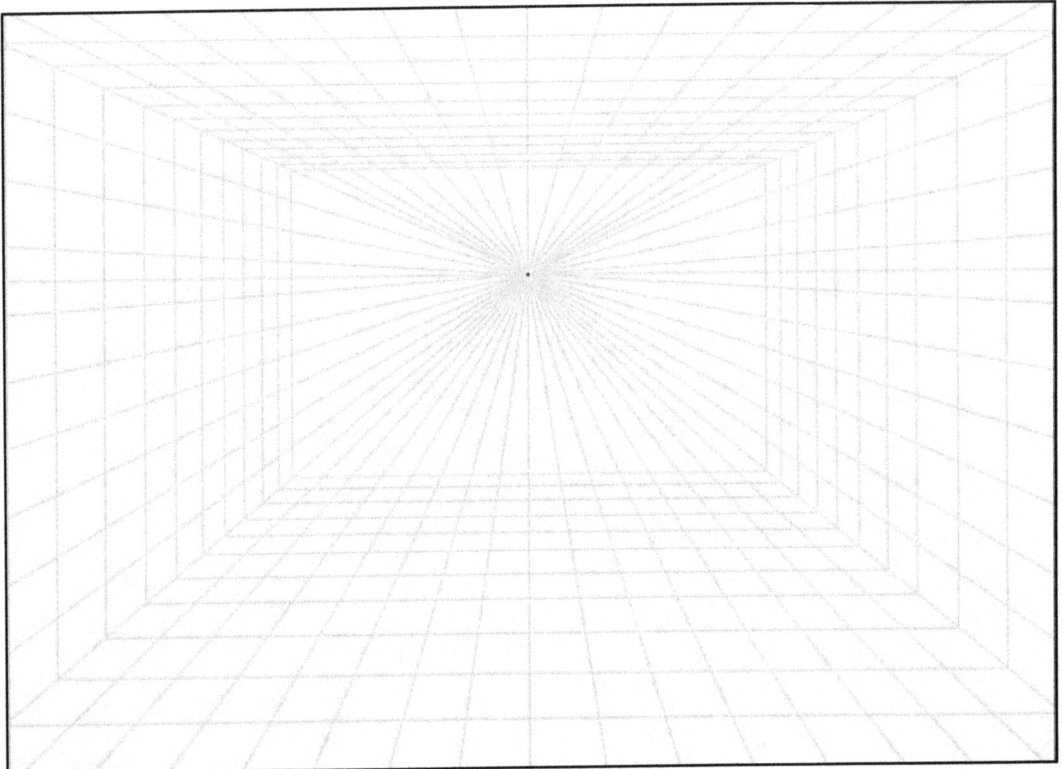

Description:

Description:

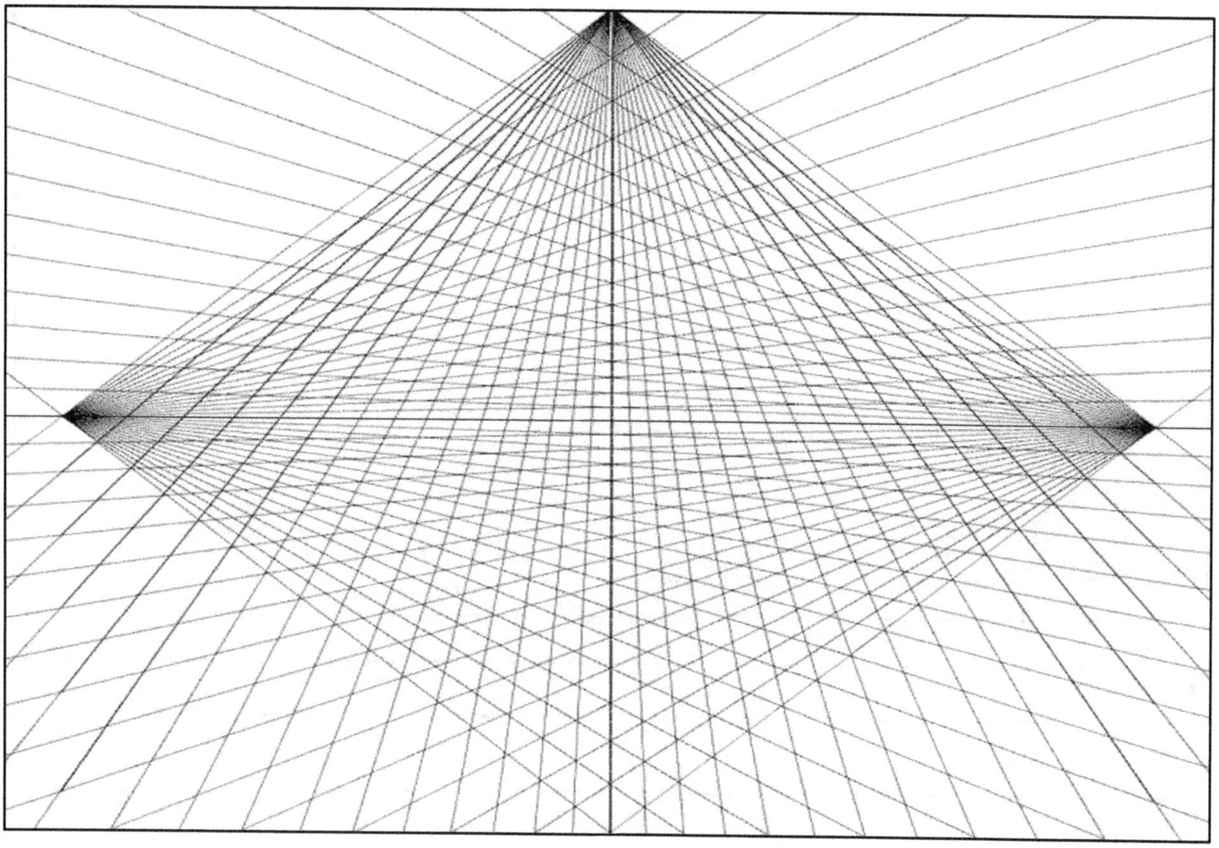

Description:

Description:

Description:

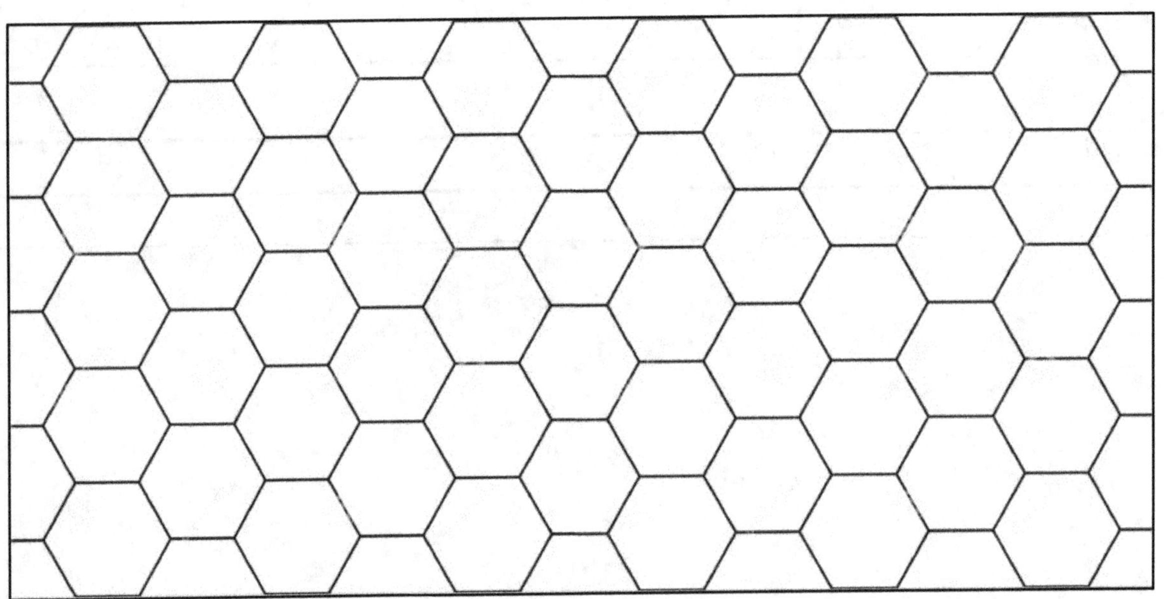

Description:

Description:

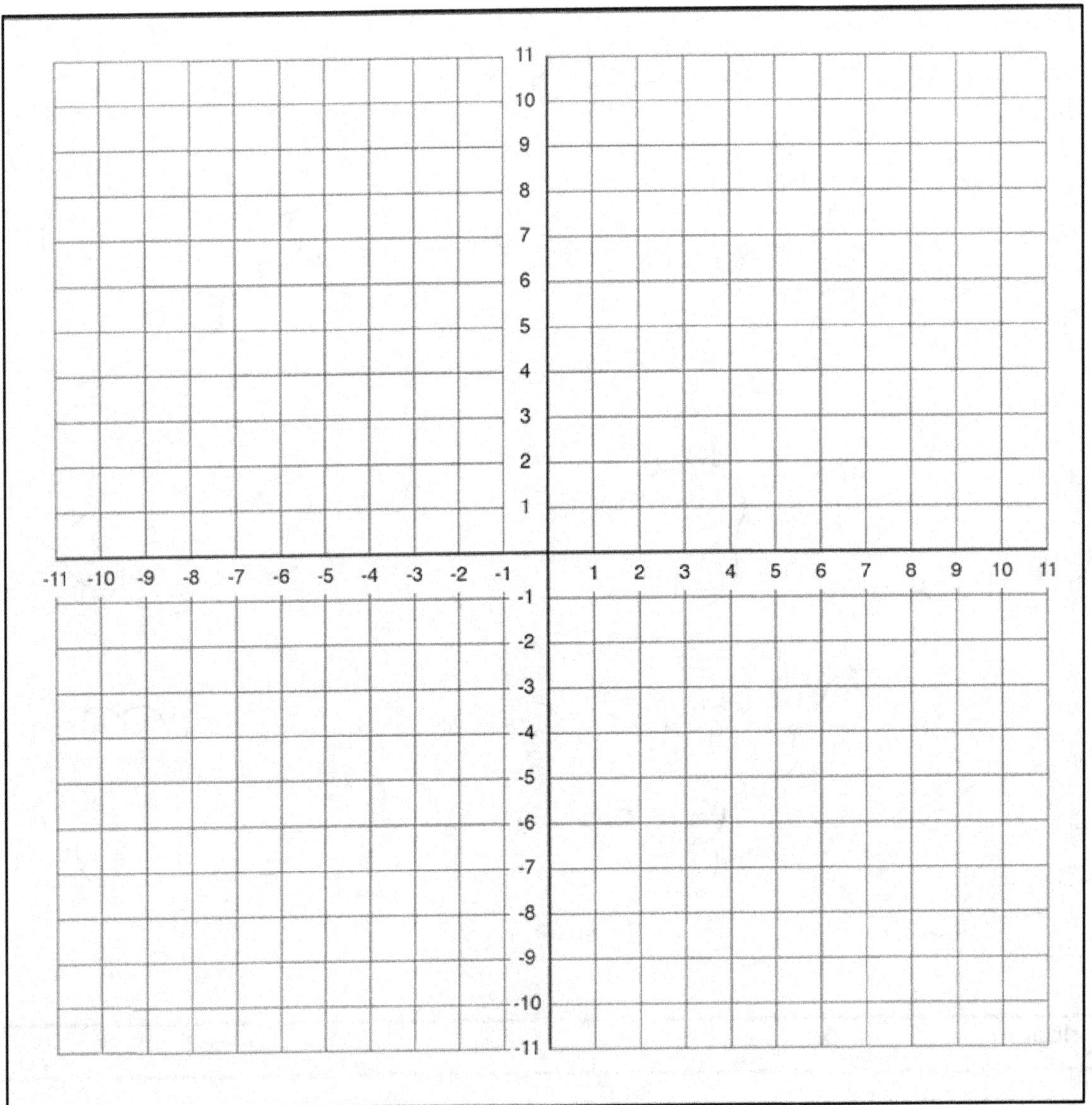

New words or phrases learned today:	Building or architectural design I like:
Ideas from a co-worker or classmate I liked:	Notes:

Description:

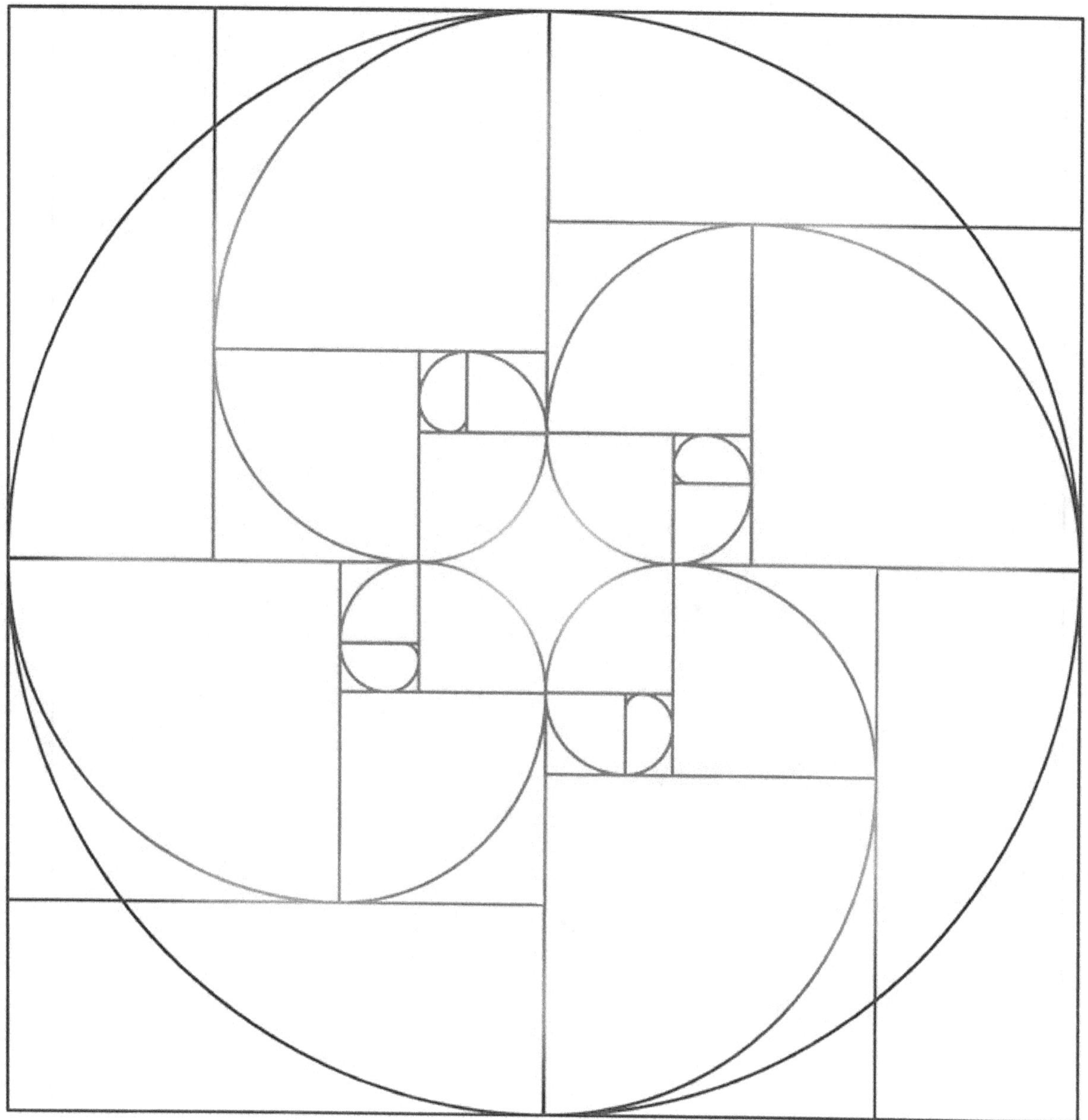

Description:

| Date: | | Day | |

Websites to Note

Need to Purchase

Simple Day Planner

New Contacts-Friends

Project Updates

Books I Want to Remember

Music I Liked

TV/Movies I Liked

Five New Ideas

Social Media Links

Twitter	
Facebook	
Instagram	
Pinterest	
Snapchat	
Other	

Other Notes

Link to Page _________

Description:

Description:

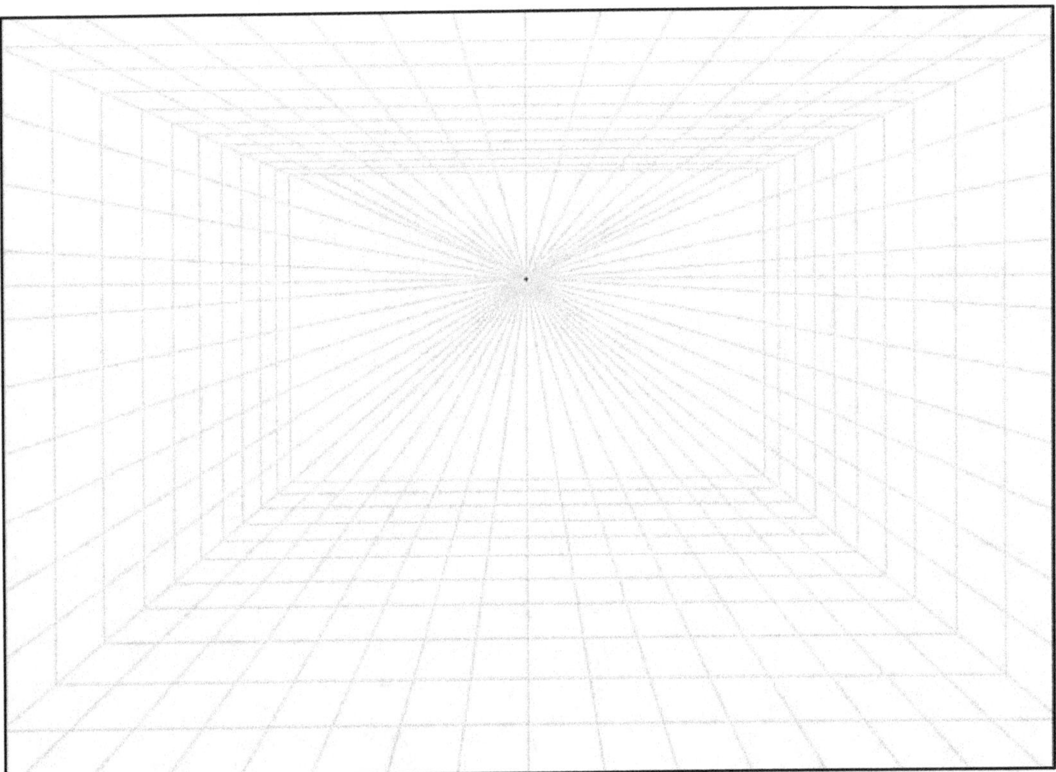

Description:

Description:

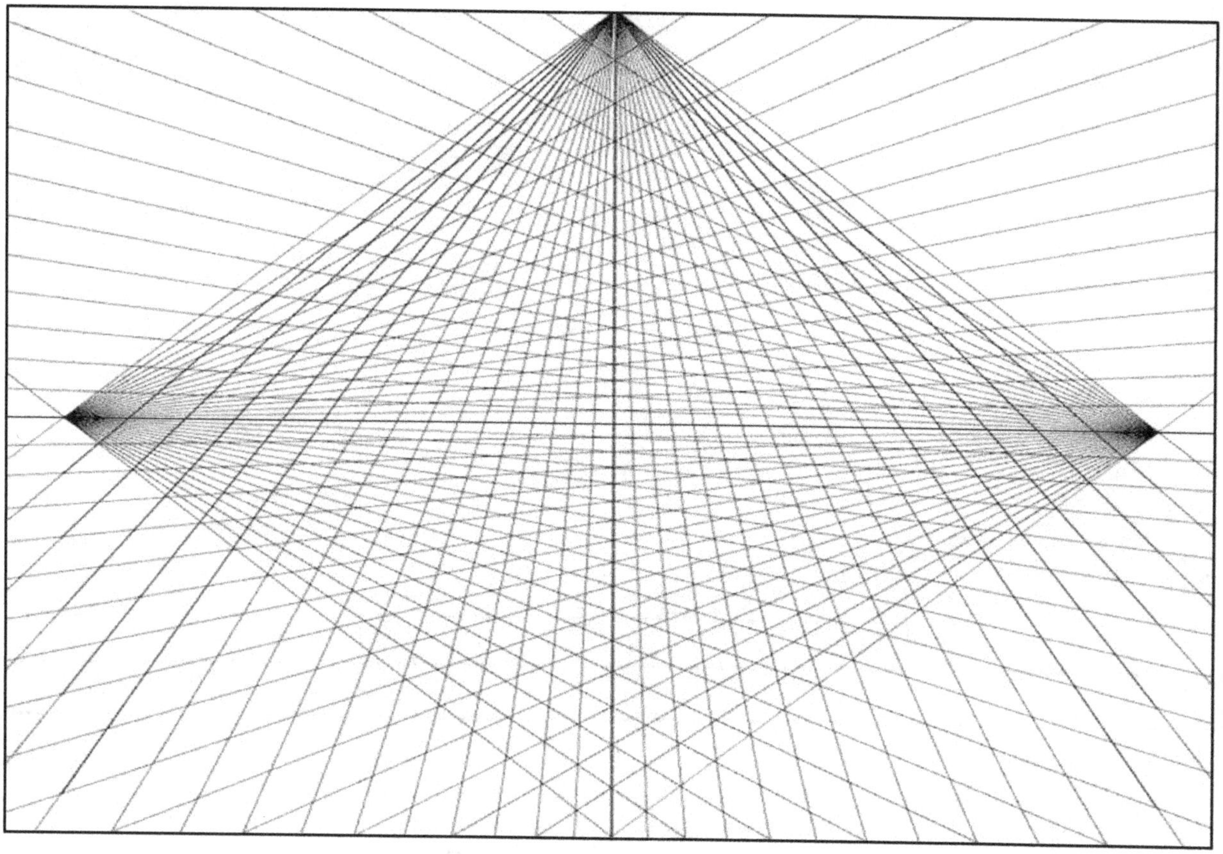

Description:

Description:

Description:

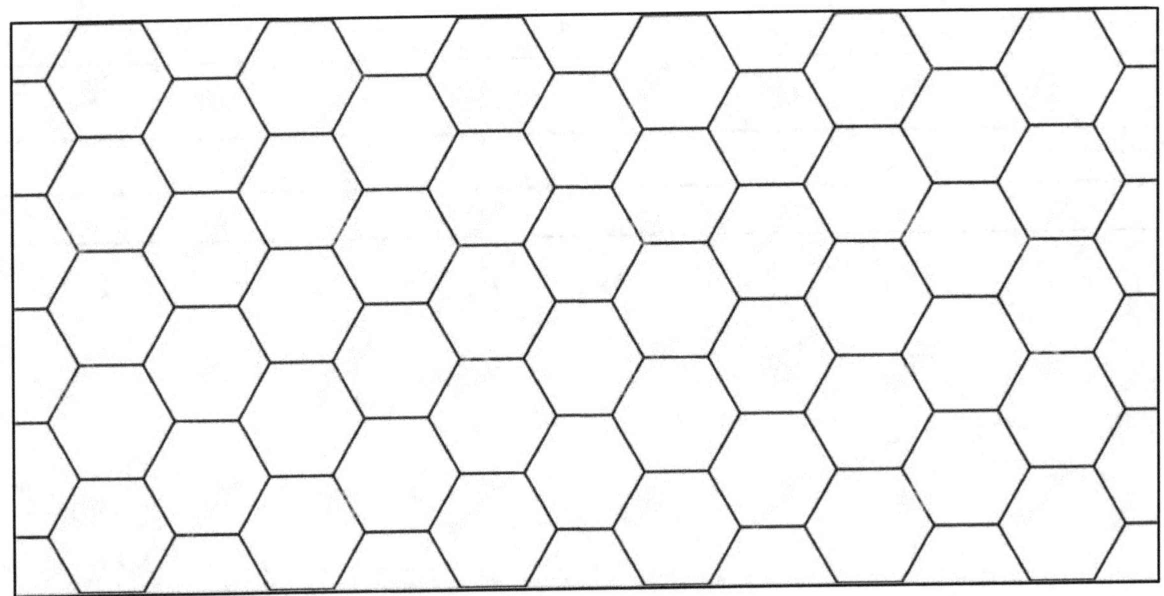

Description:

Description:

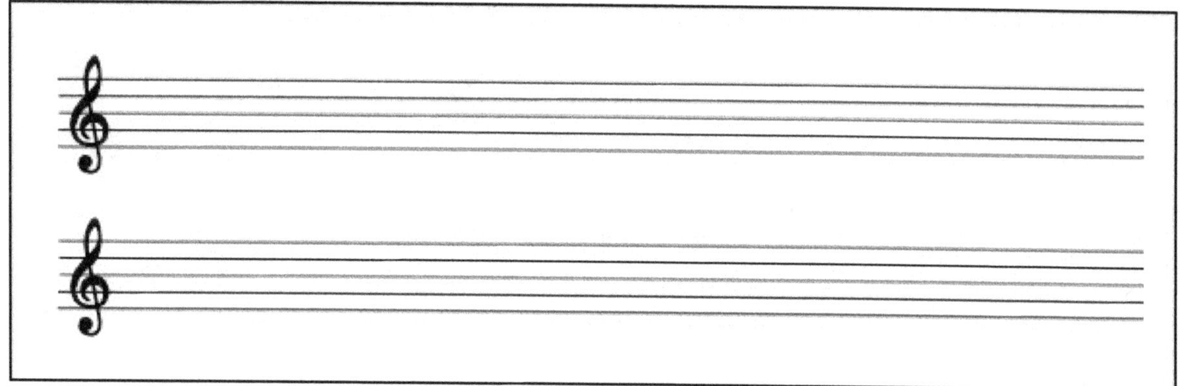

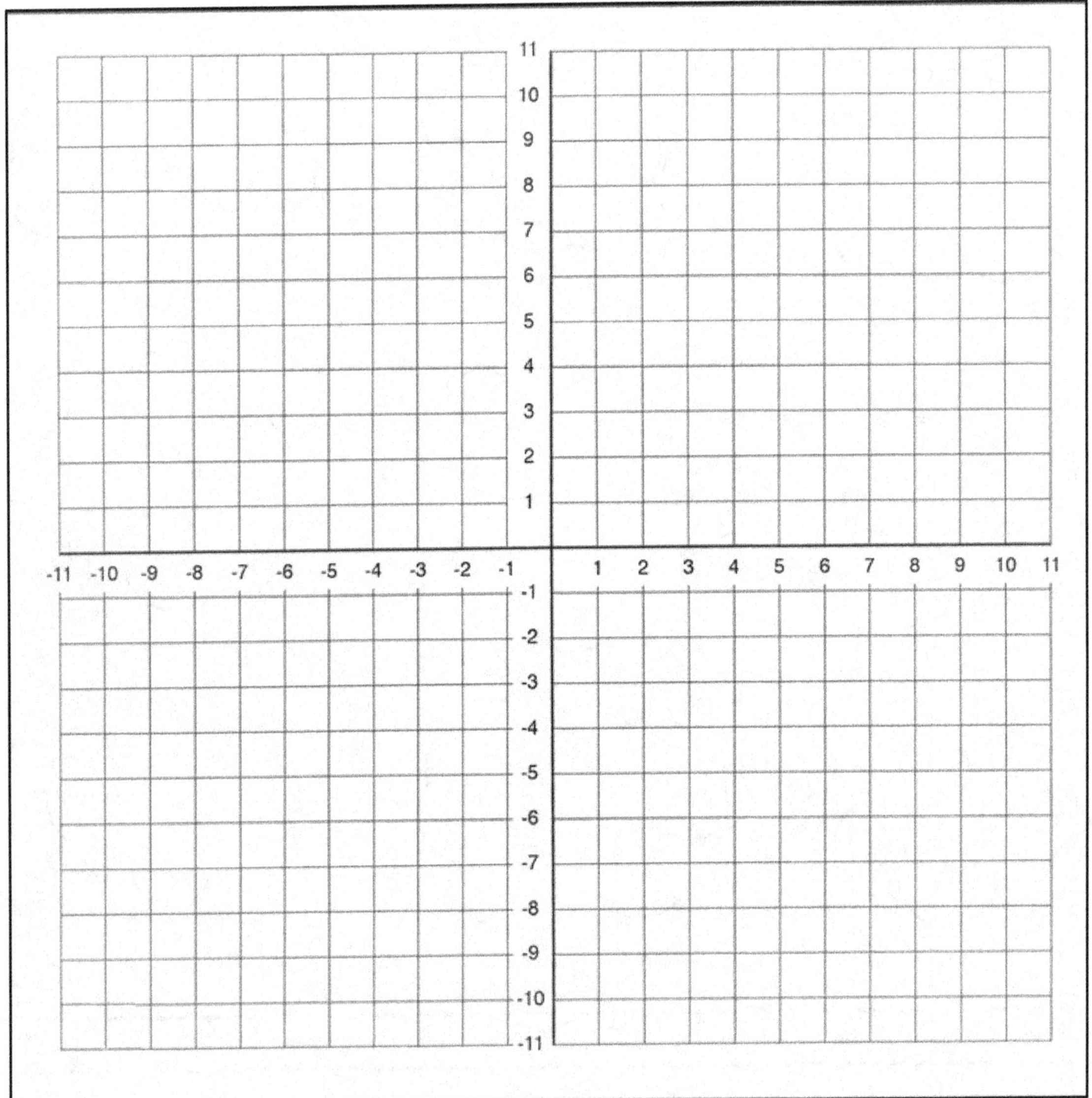

New words or phrases learned today:	Building or architectural design I like:
Ideas from a co-worker or classmate I liked:	Notes:

Description:

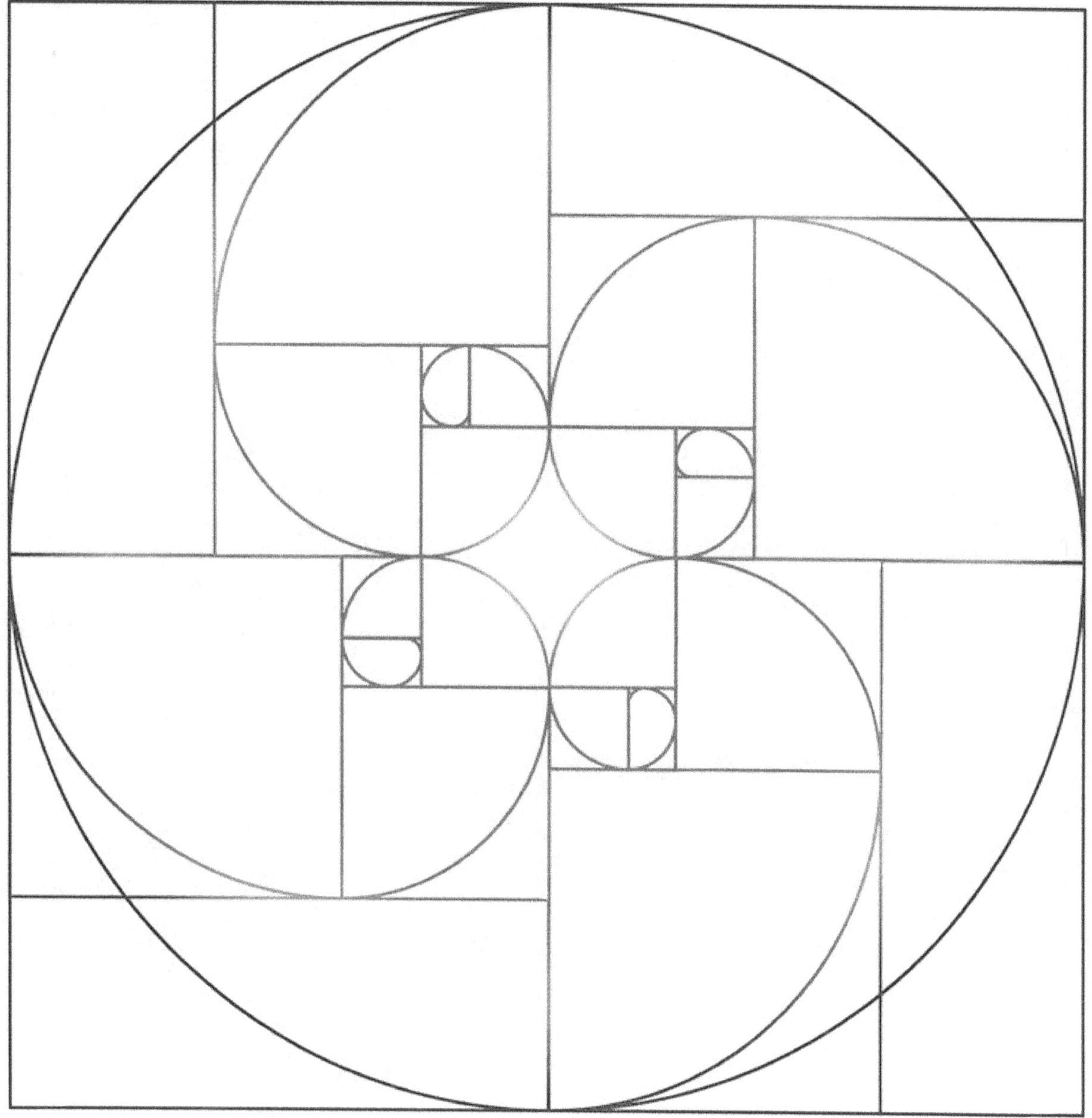

| Date: | | Day | |

Websites to Note

Simple Day Planner

Need to Purchase

New Contacts-Friends

Books I Want to Remember

Music I Liked

Project Updates

TV/Movies I Liked

Five New Ideas

Social Media Links

Twitter	
Facebook	
Instagram	
Pinterest	
Snapchat	
Other	

Other Notes

Link to Page _________

Description:

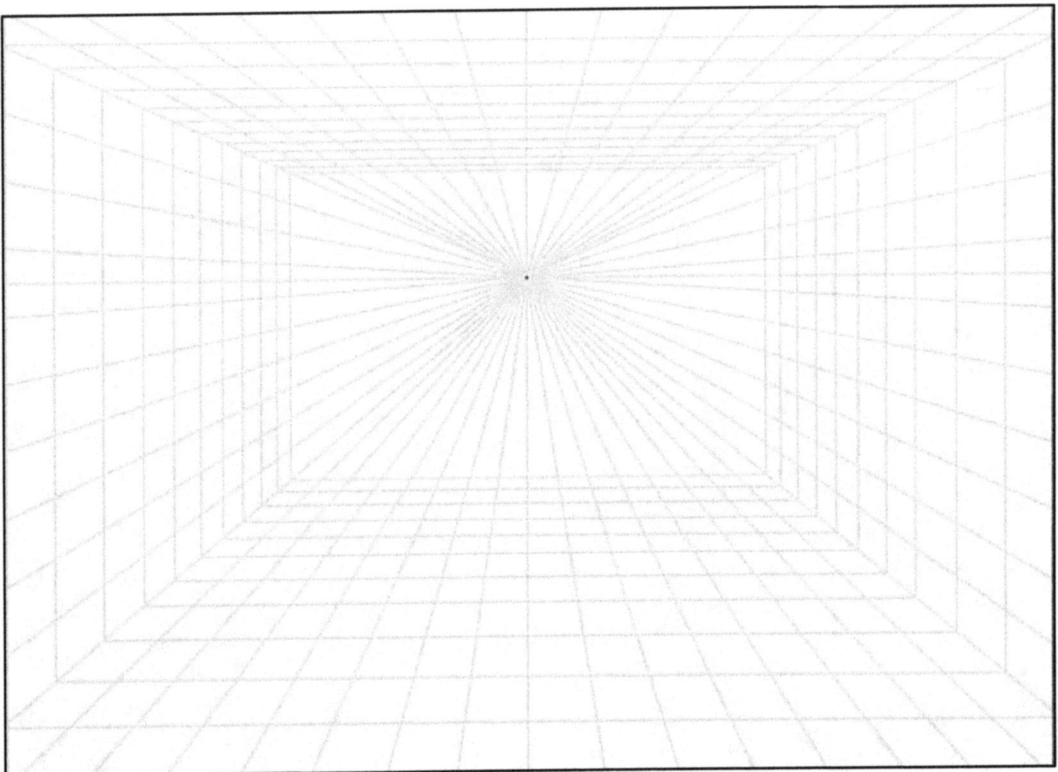

Description:

Description:

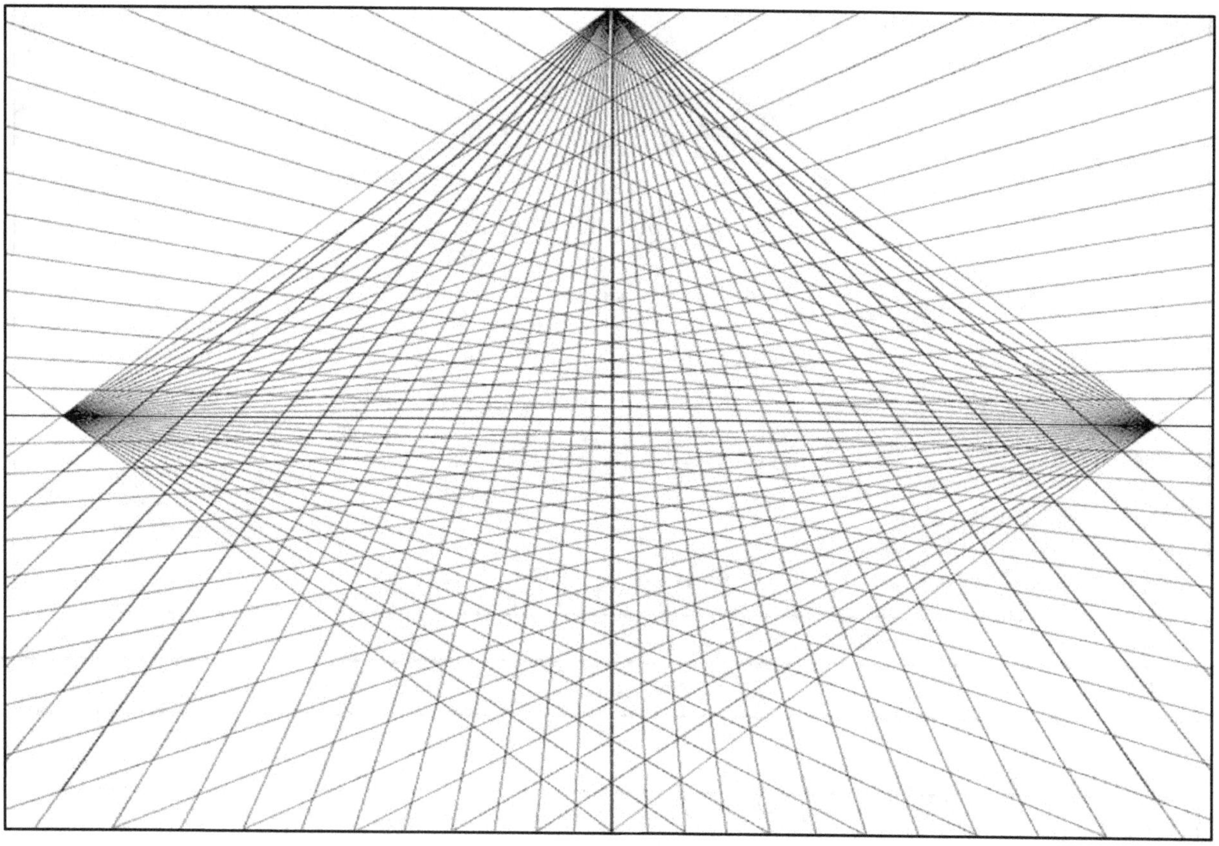

Description:

Description:

Description:

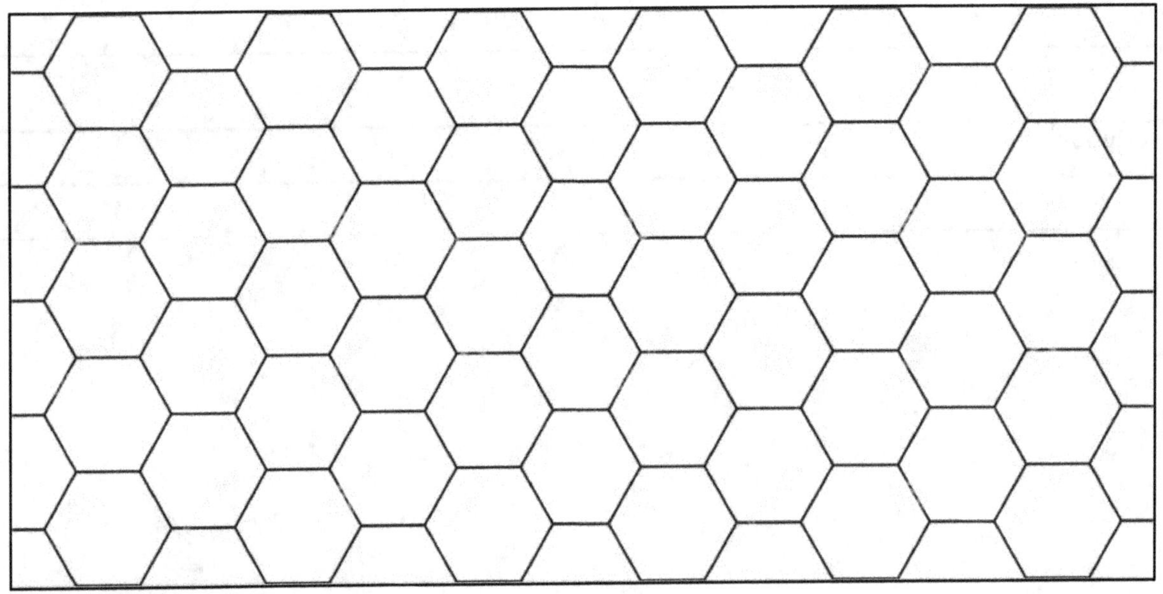

Description:

Description:

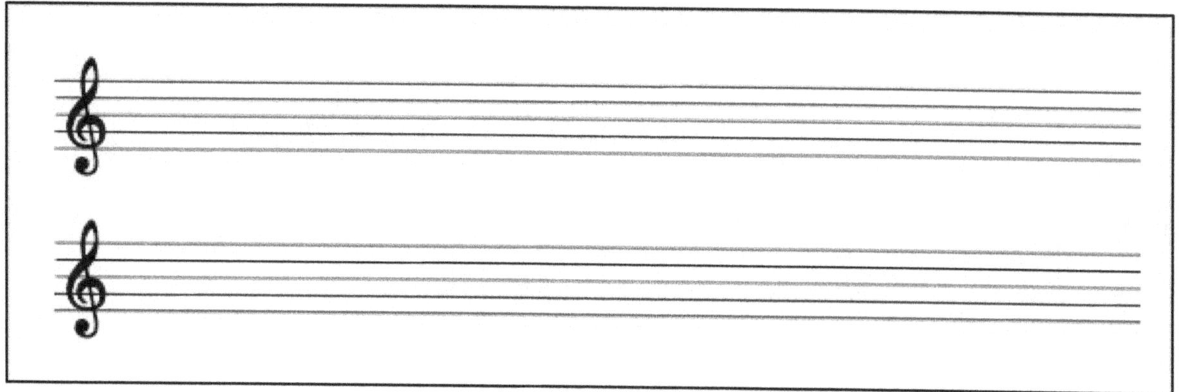

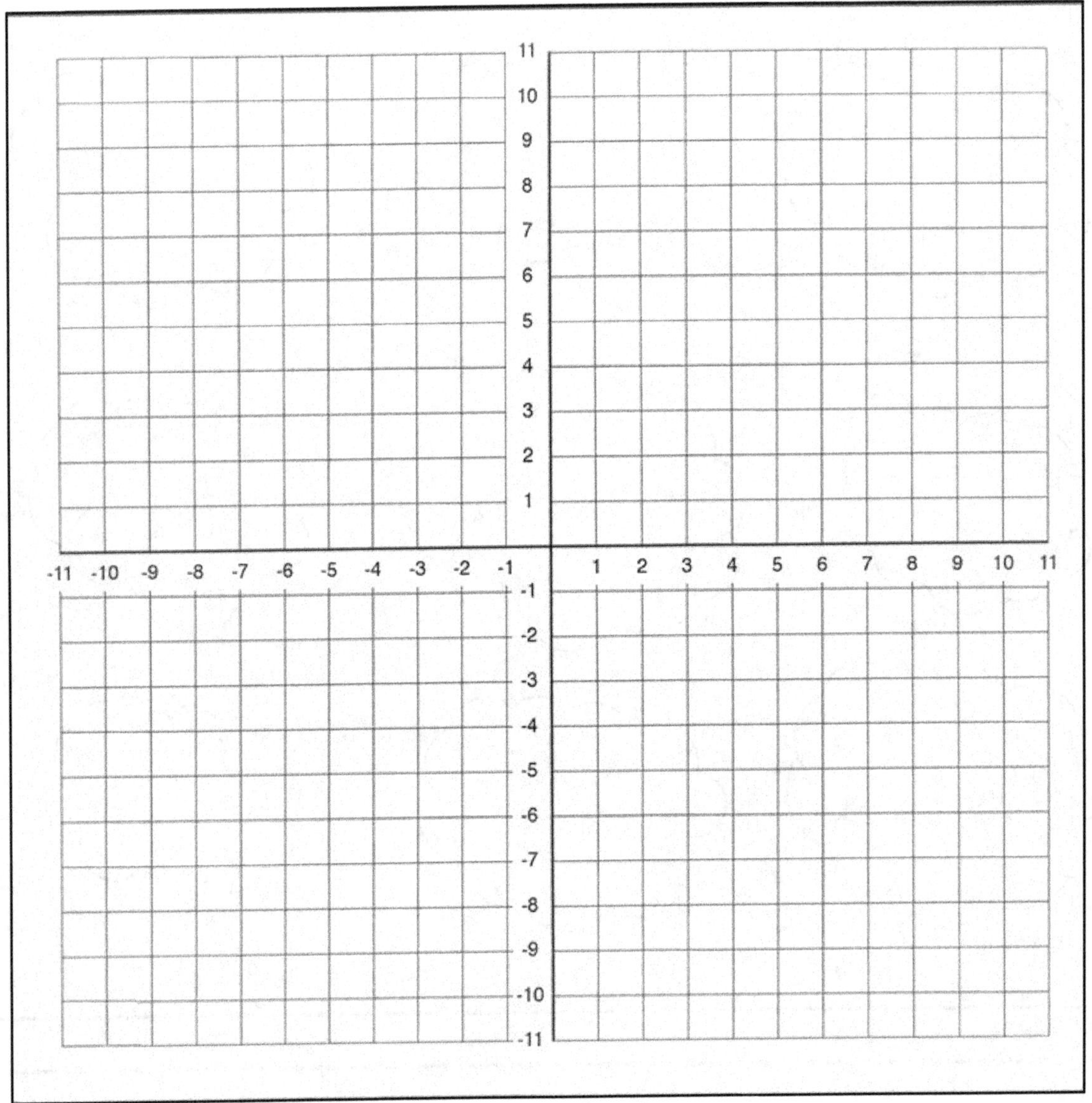

New words or phrases learned today:	Building or architectural design I like:
Ideas from a co-worker or classmate I liked:	Notes:

Description:

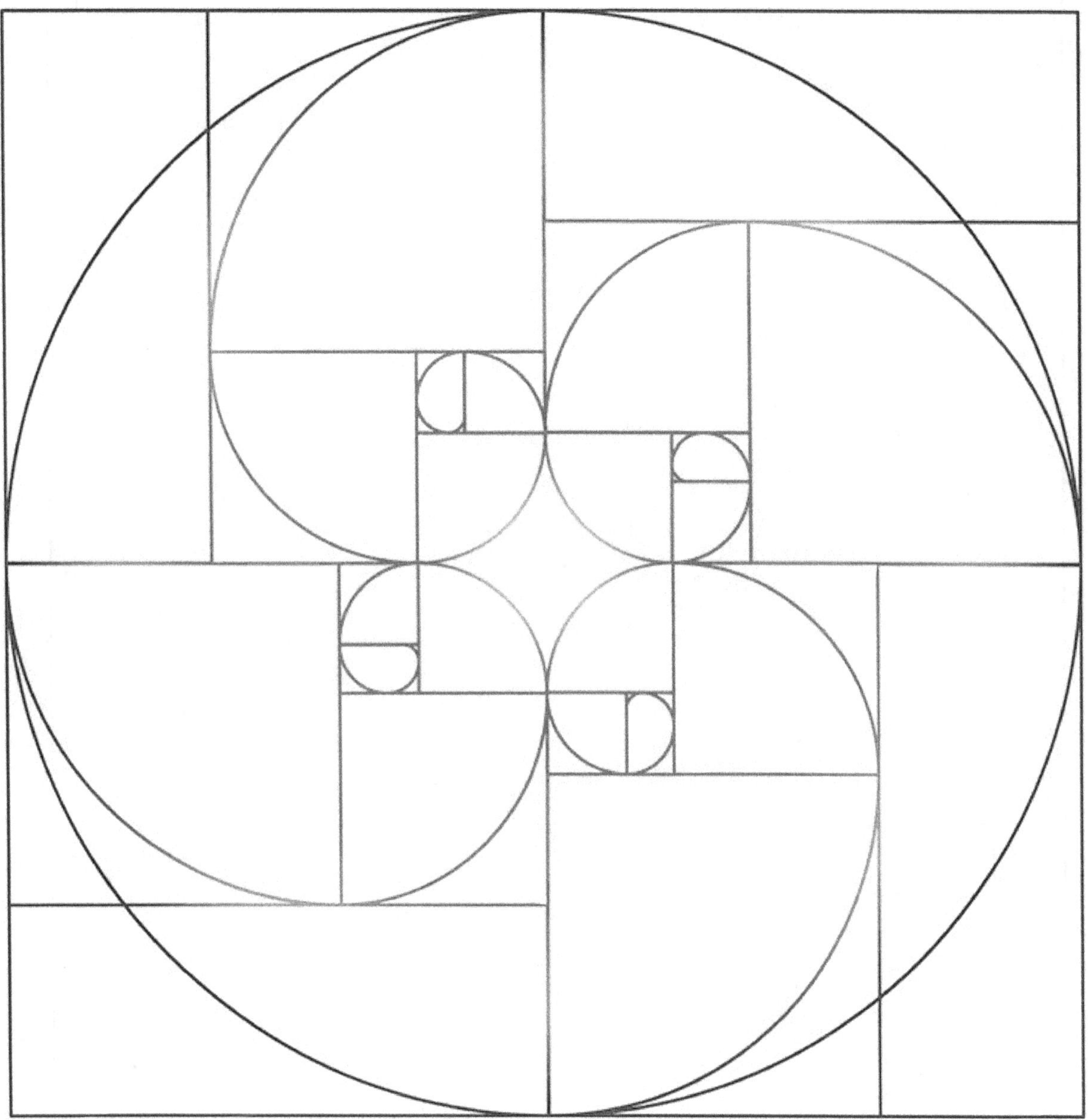

<table>
<tr><td>Date:</td><td></td><td>Day</td><td></td></tr>
</table>

Websites to Note

Simple Day Planner

Need to Purchase

New Contacts-Friends

Books I Want to Remember

Music I Liked

Project Updates

TV/Movies I Liked

Five New Ideas

Social Media Links

Twitter	
Facebook	
Instagram	
Pinterest	
Snapchat	
Other	

Other Notes

Link to Page __________

Description:

Description:

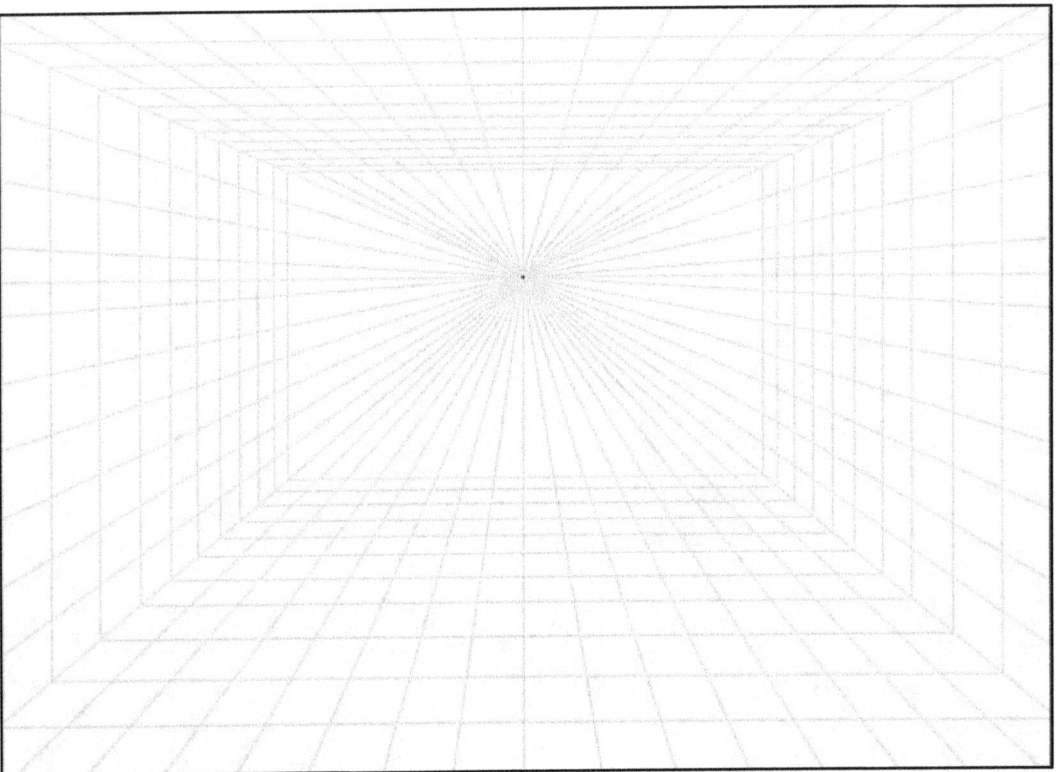

Description:

Description:

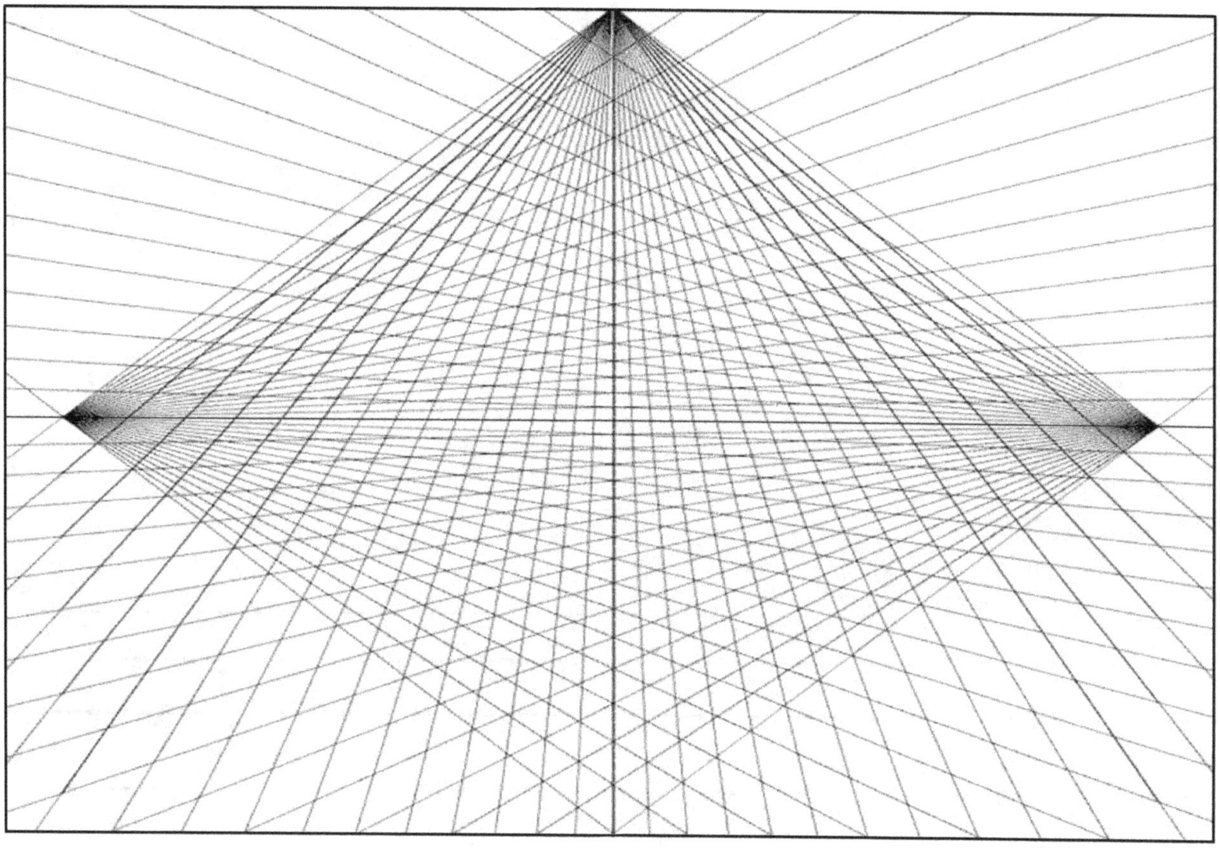

Description:

Description:

Description:

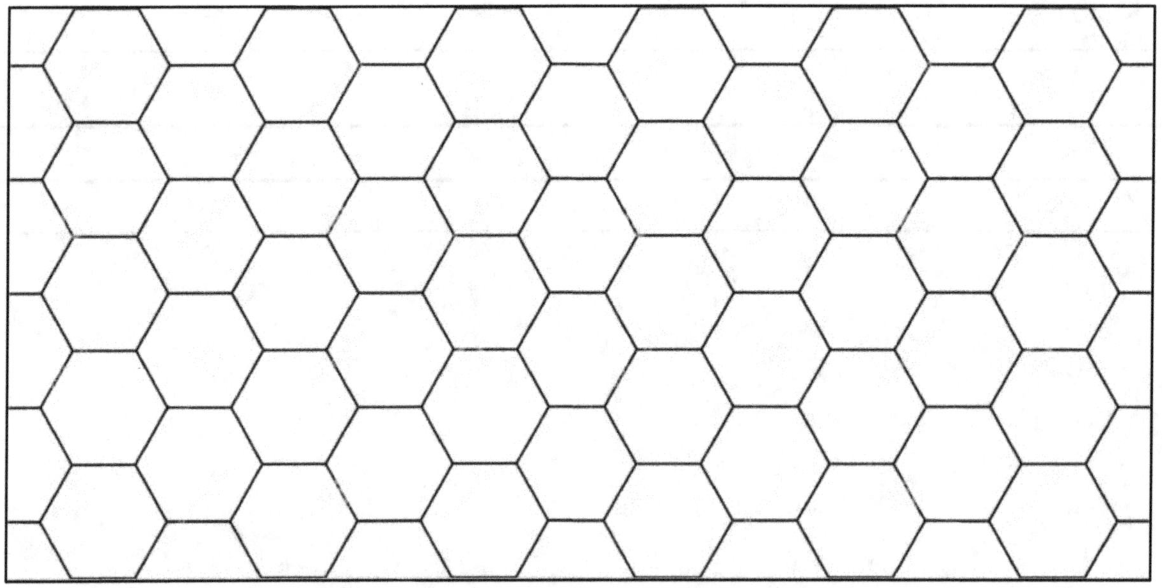

Description:

Description:

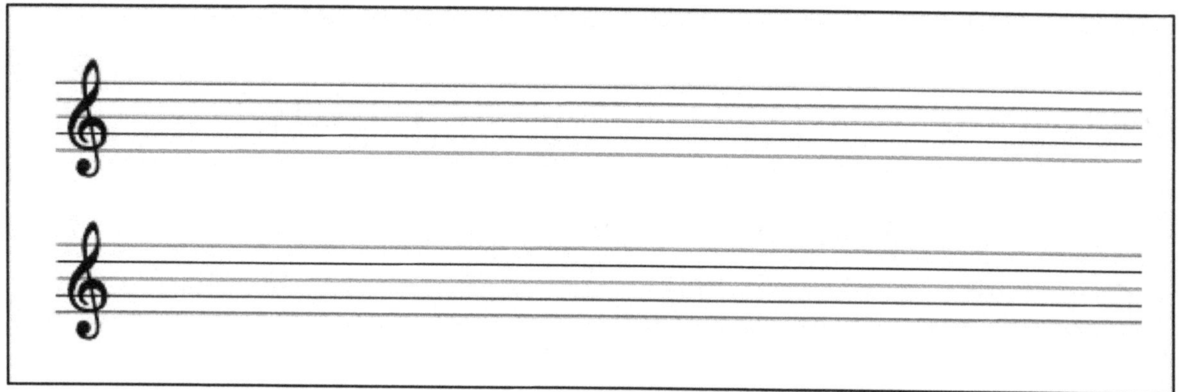

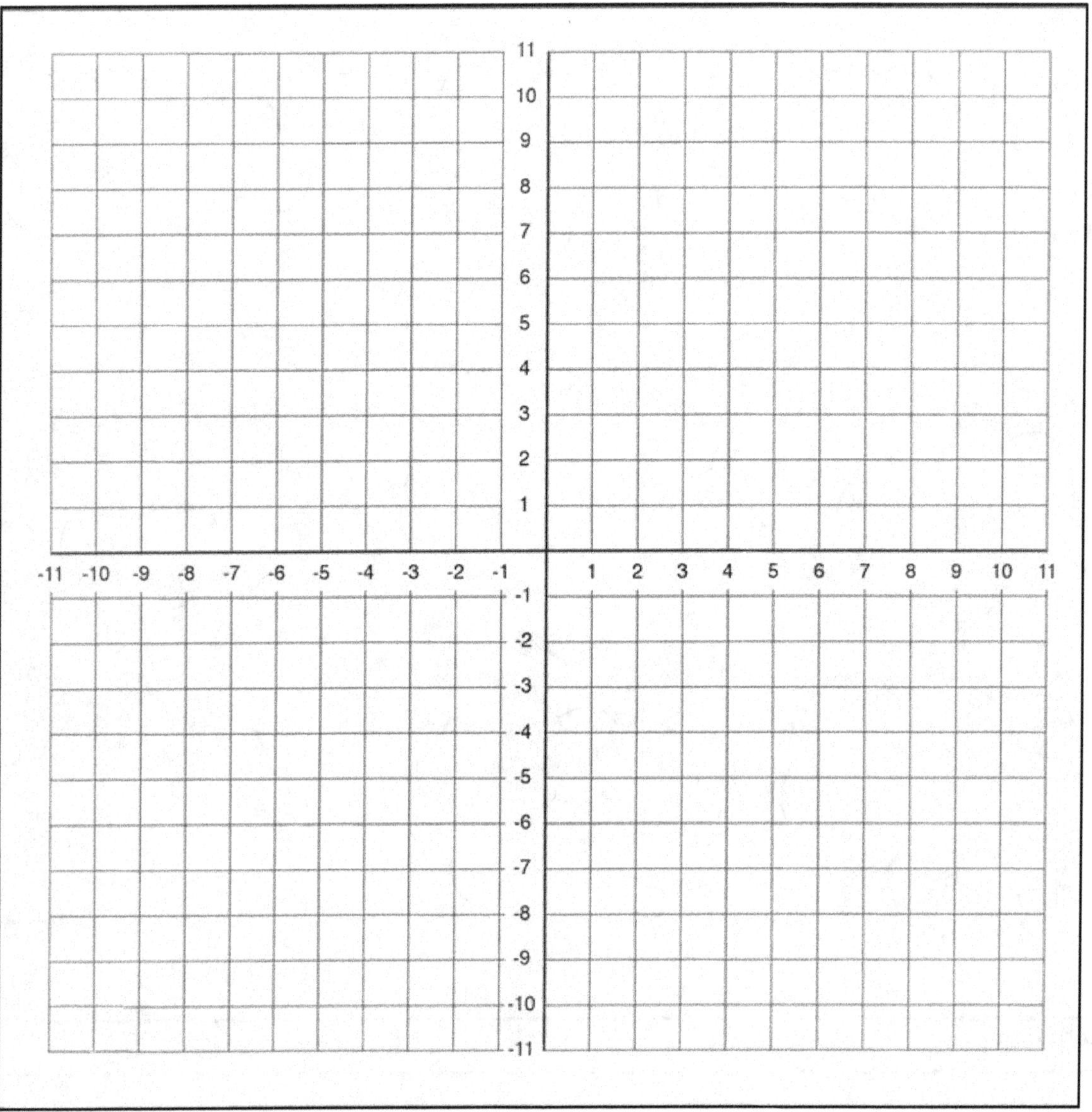

New words or phrases learned today:	Building or architectural design I like:
Ideas from a co-worker or classmate I liked:	Notes:

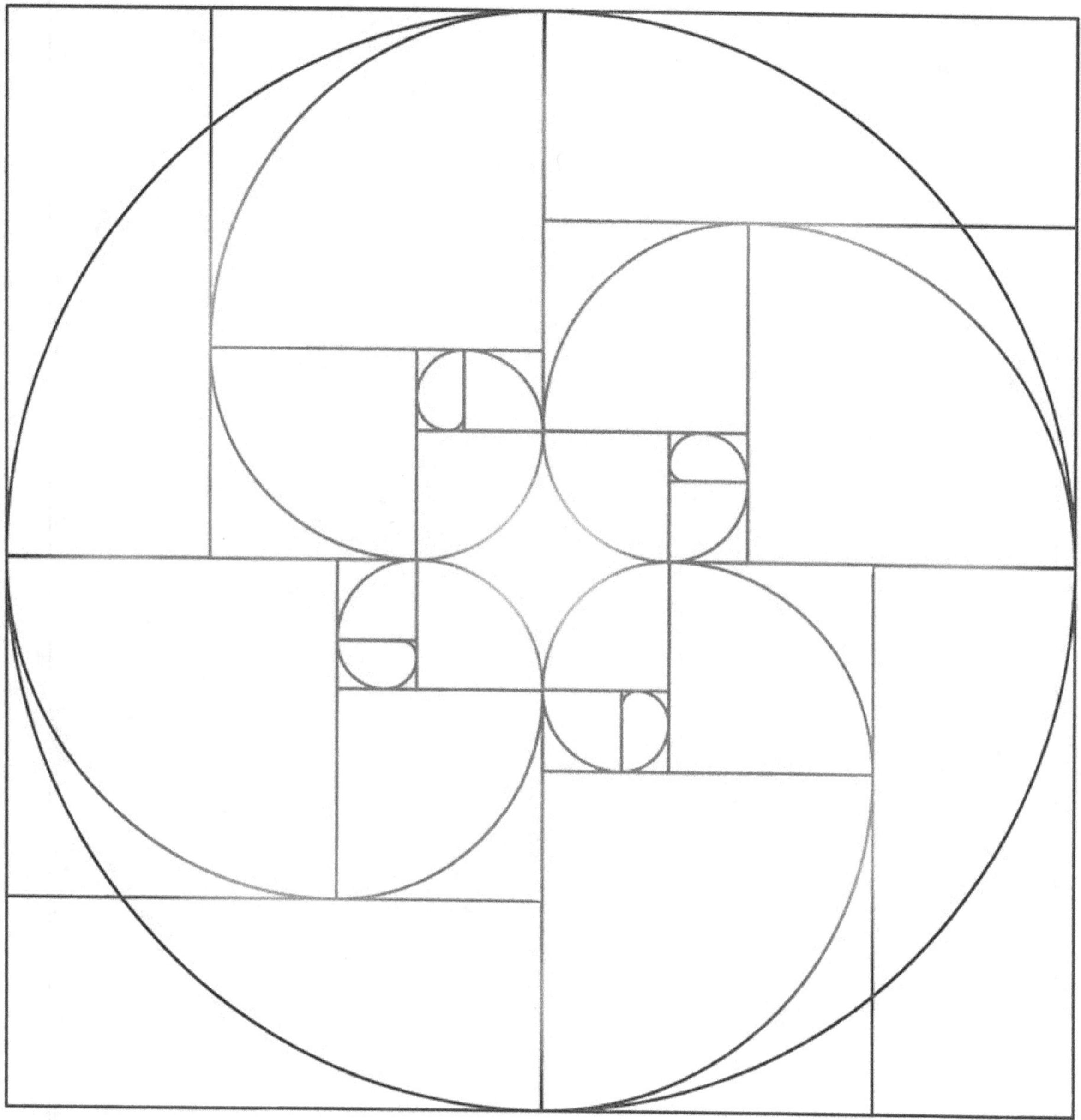

| Date: | | Day | |

Websites to Note

Need to Purchase

Simple Day Planner

New Contacts-Friends

Project Updates

Books I Want to Remember

Music I Liked

TV/Movies I Liked

Five New Ideas

Social Media Links

Twitter	
Facebook	
Instagram	
Pinterest	
Snapchat	
Other	

Other Notes

Link to Page __________

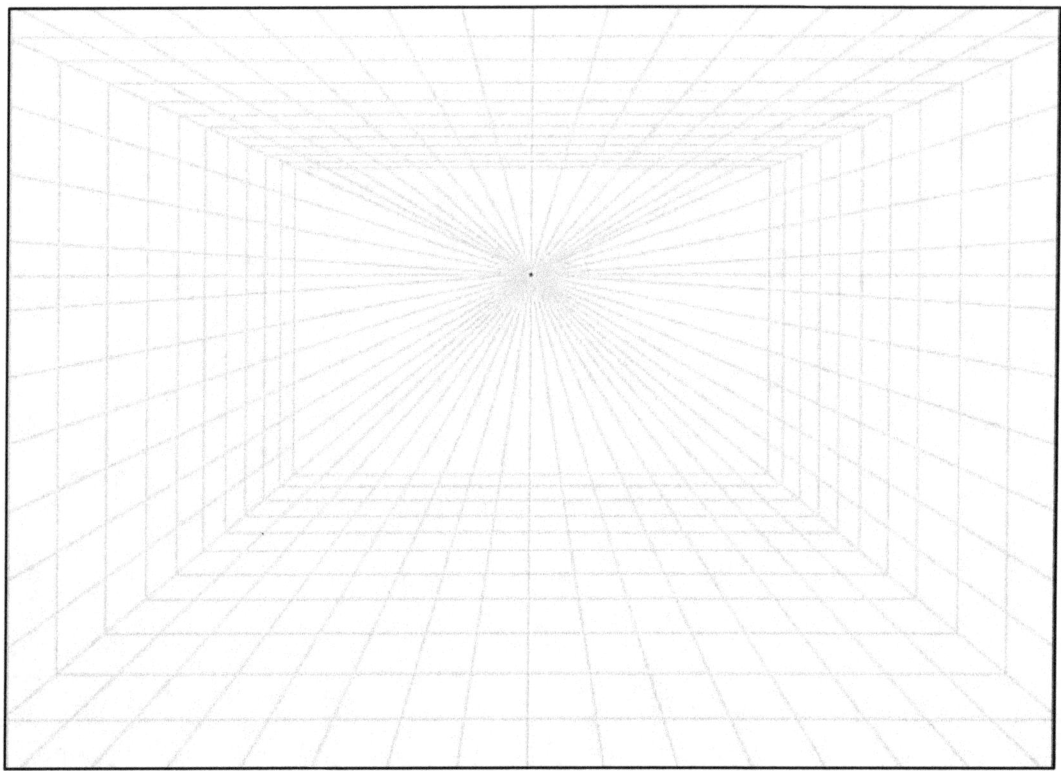

Description:

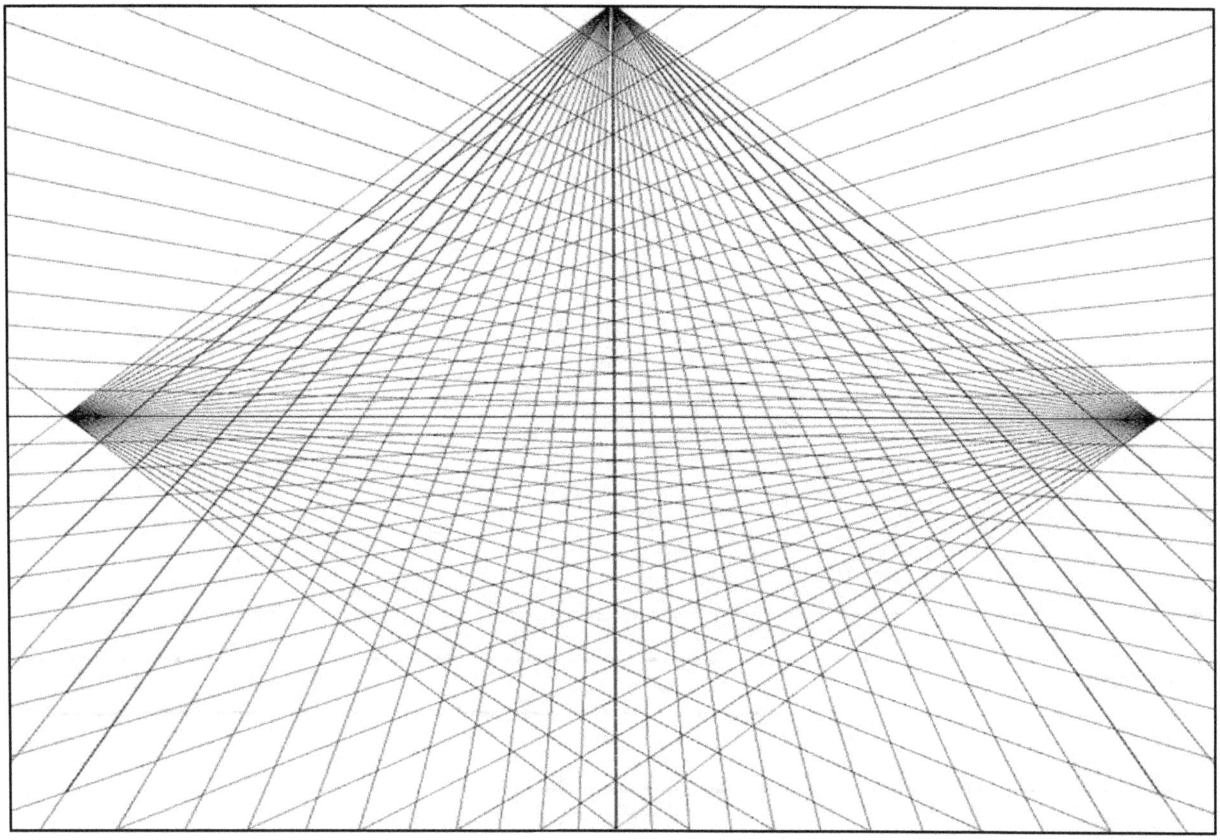

Description:

Description:

Description:

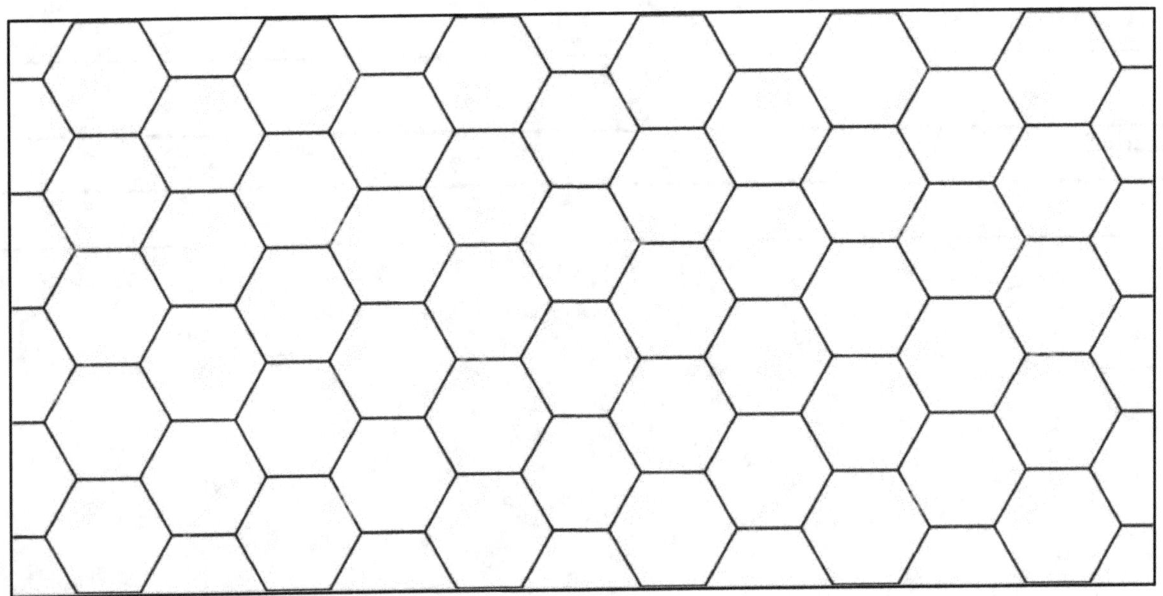

Description:

Description:

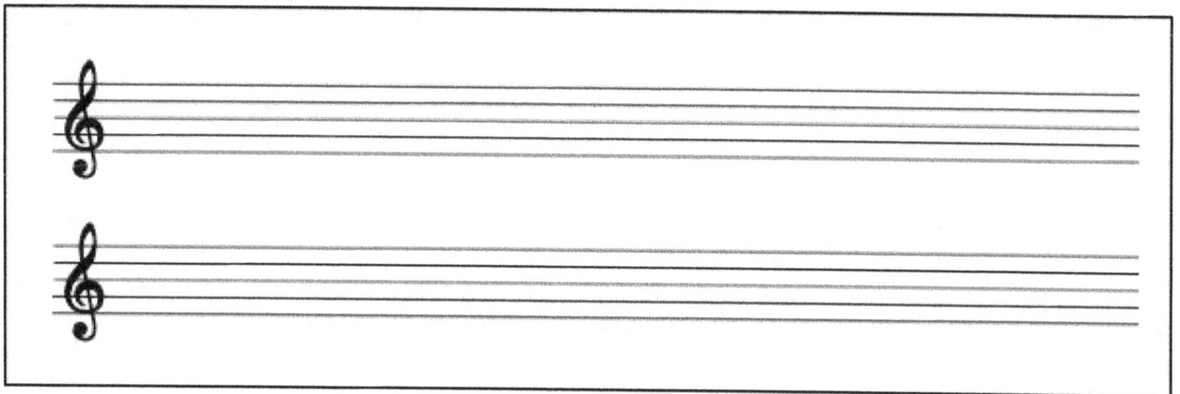

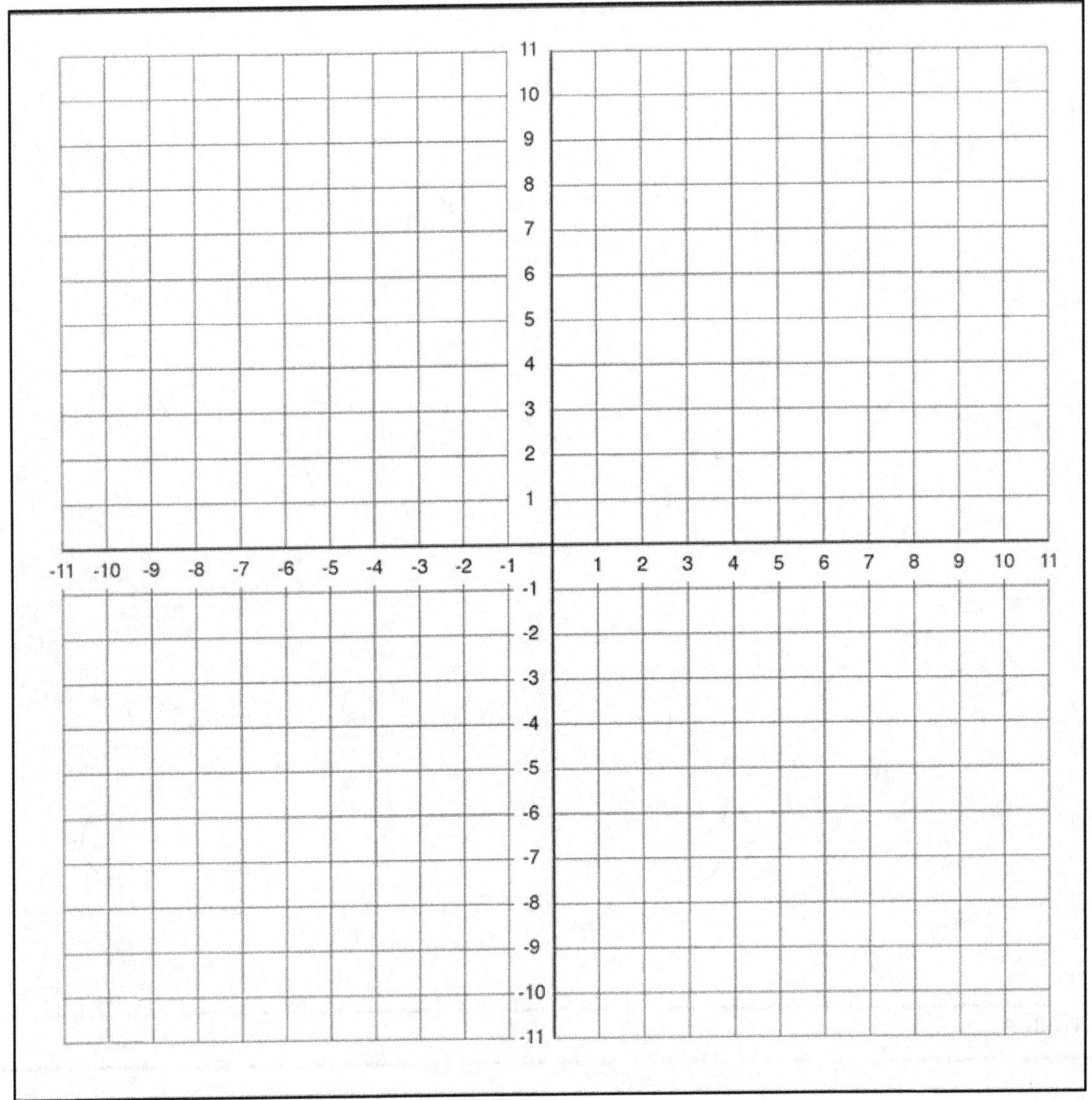

New words or phrases learned today:	Building or architectural design I like:
Ideas from a co-worker or classmate I liked:	Notes:

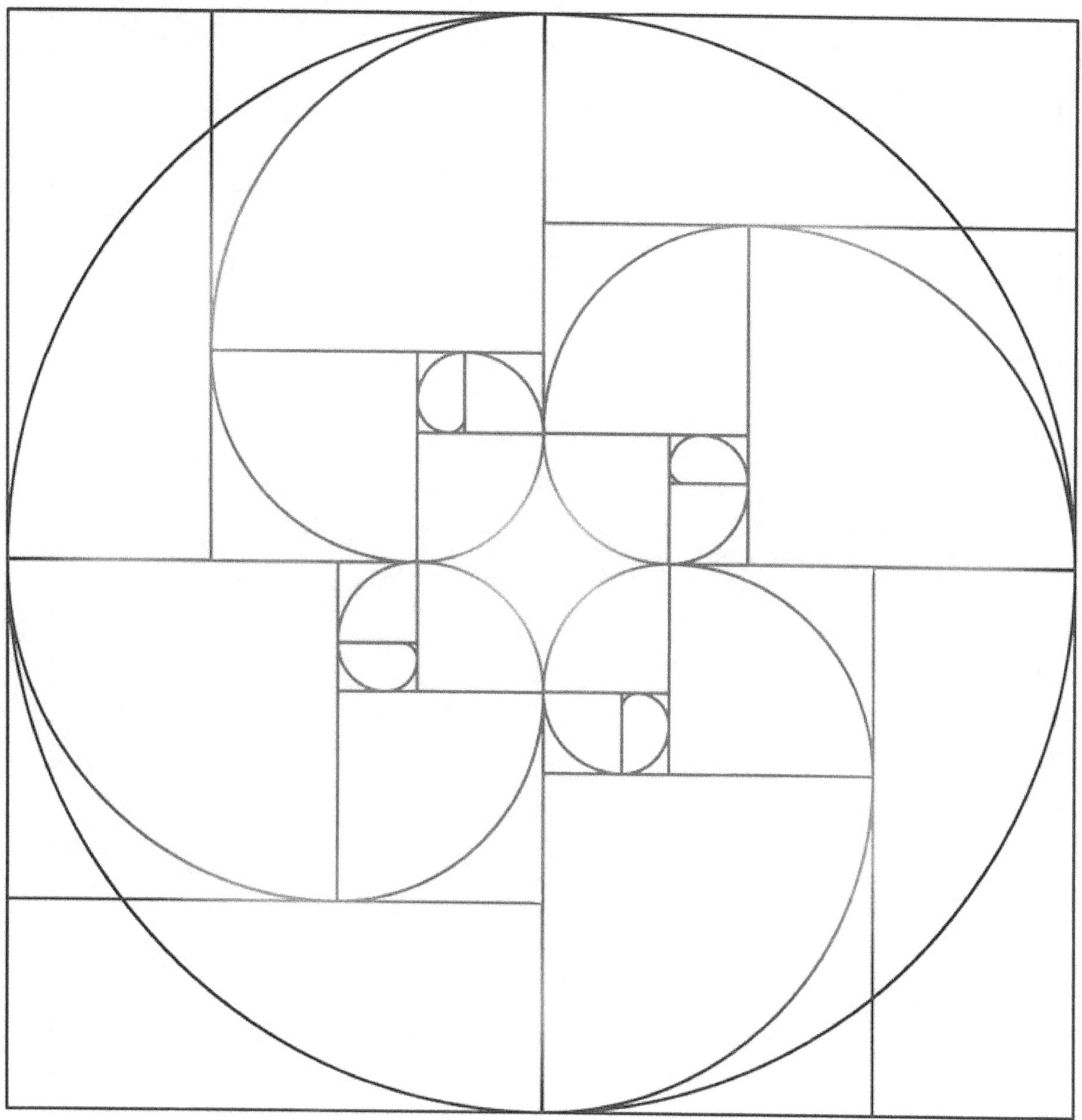

Date: | Day

Websites to Note

Need to Purchase

Simple Day Planner

New Contacts-Friends

Project Updates

Books I Want to Remember

Music I Liked

TV/Movies I Liked

Five New Ideas

Social Media Links

Twitter
Facebook
Instagram
Pinterest
Snapchat
Other

Other Notes

Link to Page _________

Description:

Description:

Description:

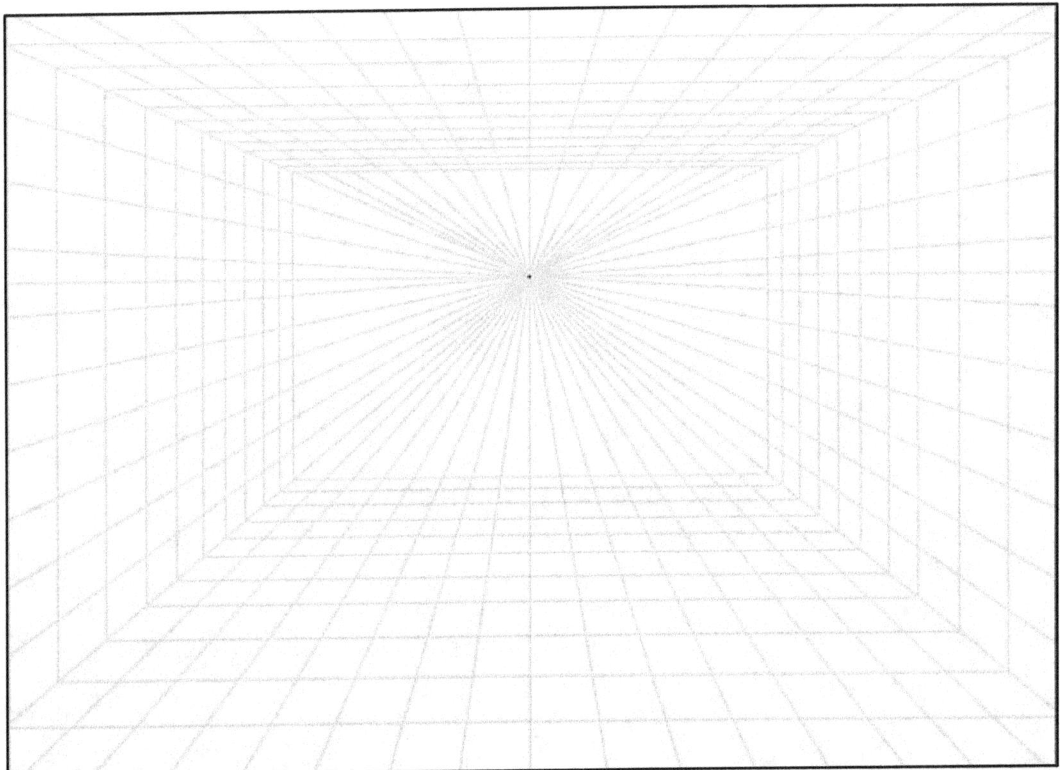

Description:

[166]

Description:

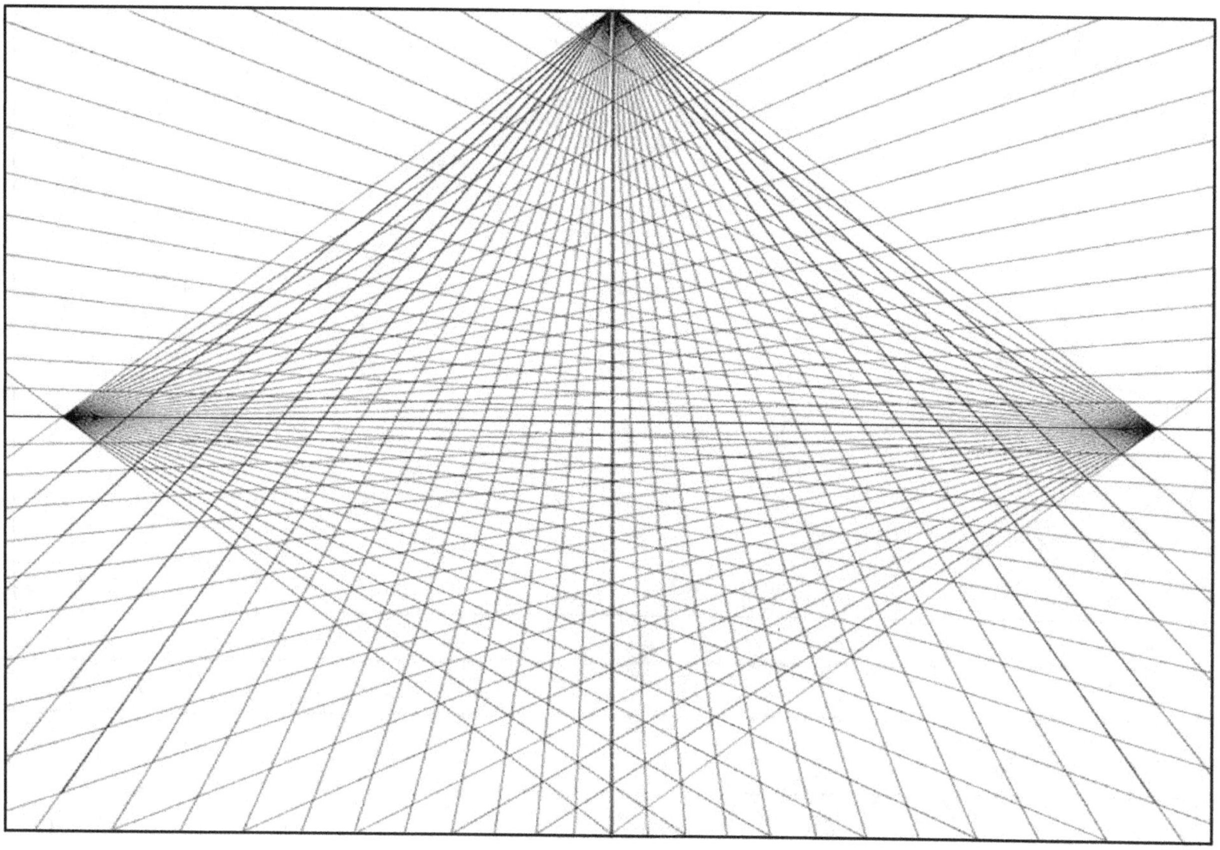

Description:

Description:

Description:

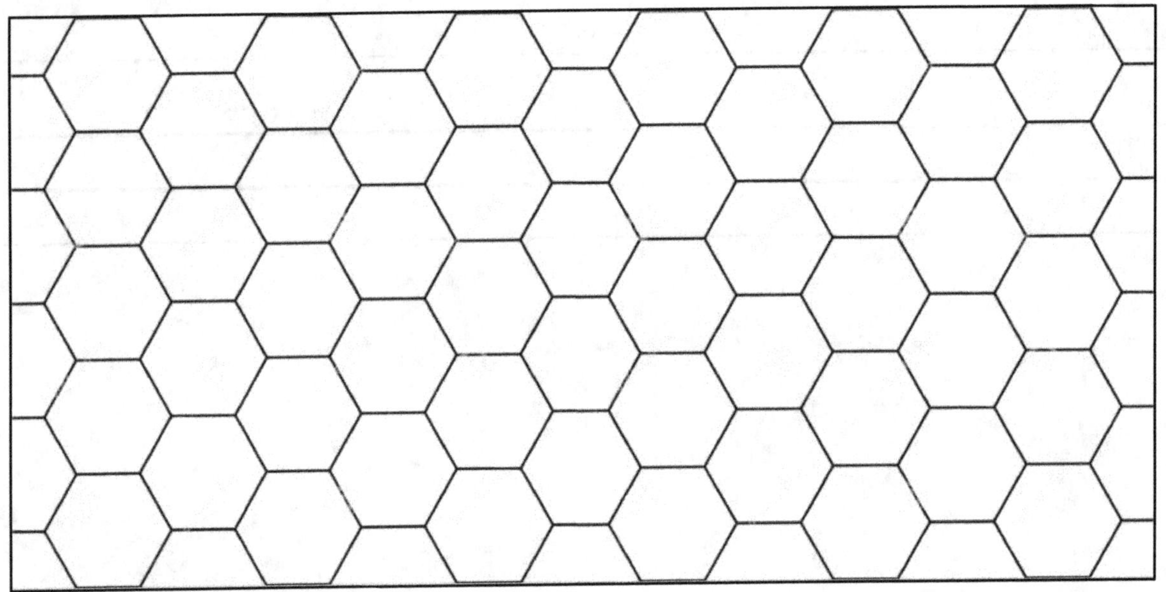

Description:

Description:

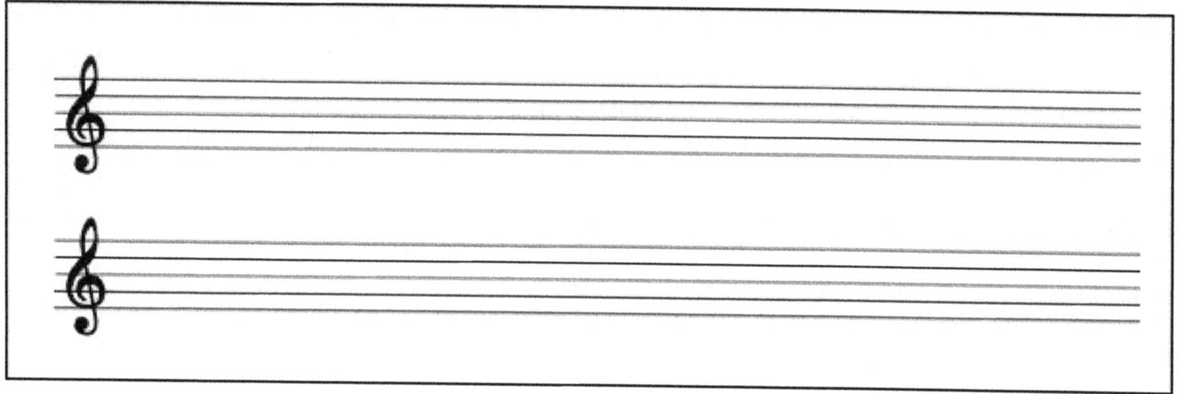

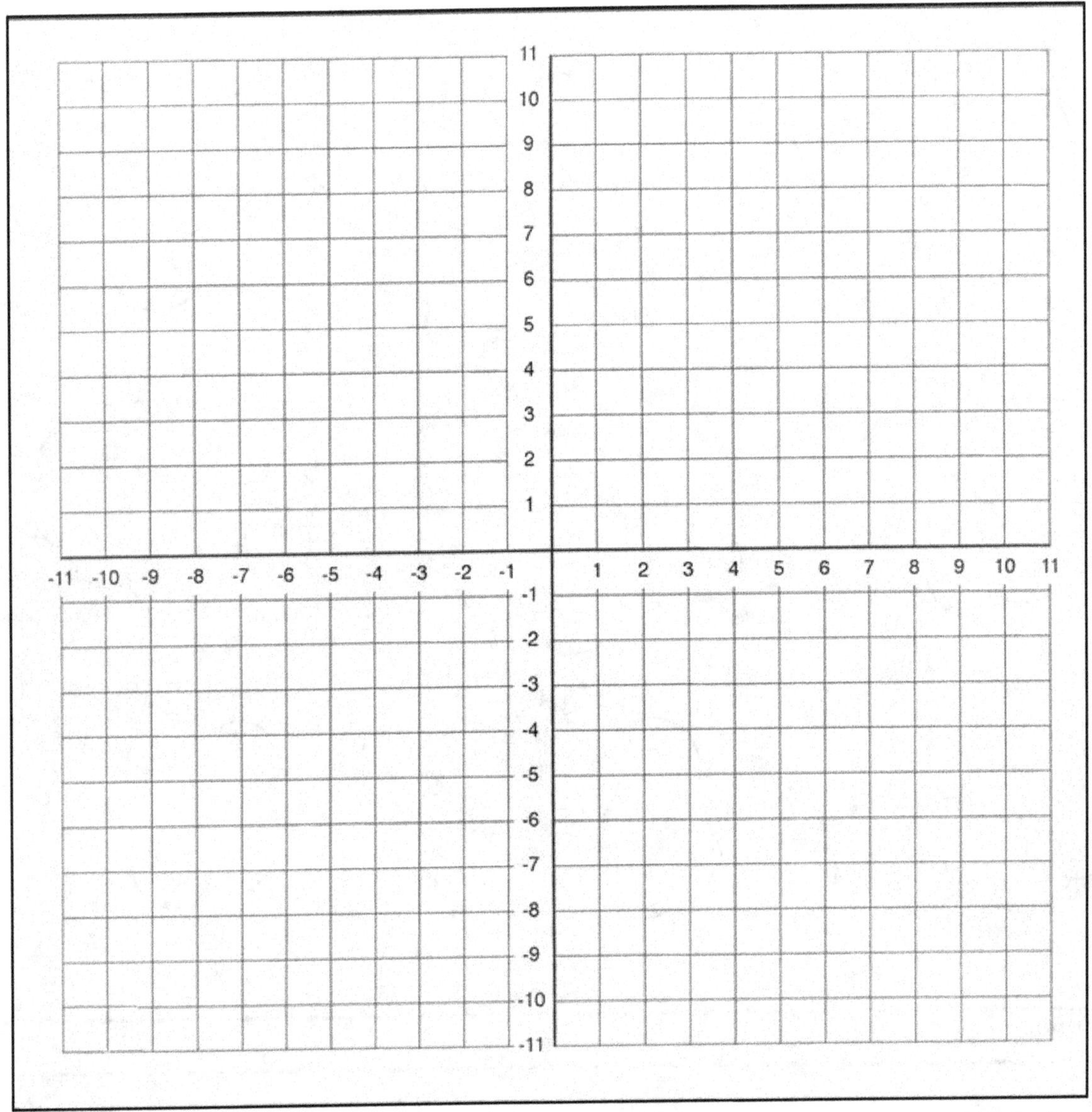

New words or phrases learned today:	Building or architectural design I like:
Ideas from a co-worker or classmate I liked:	Notes:

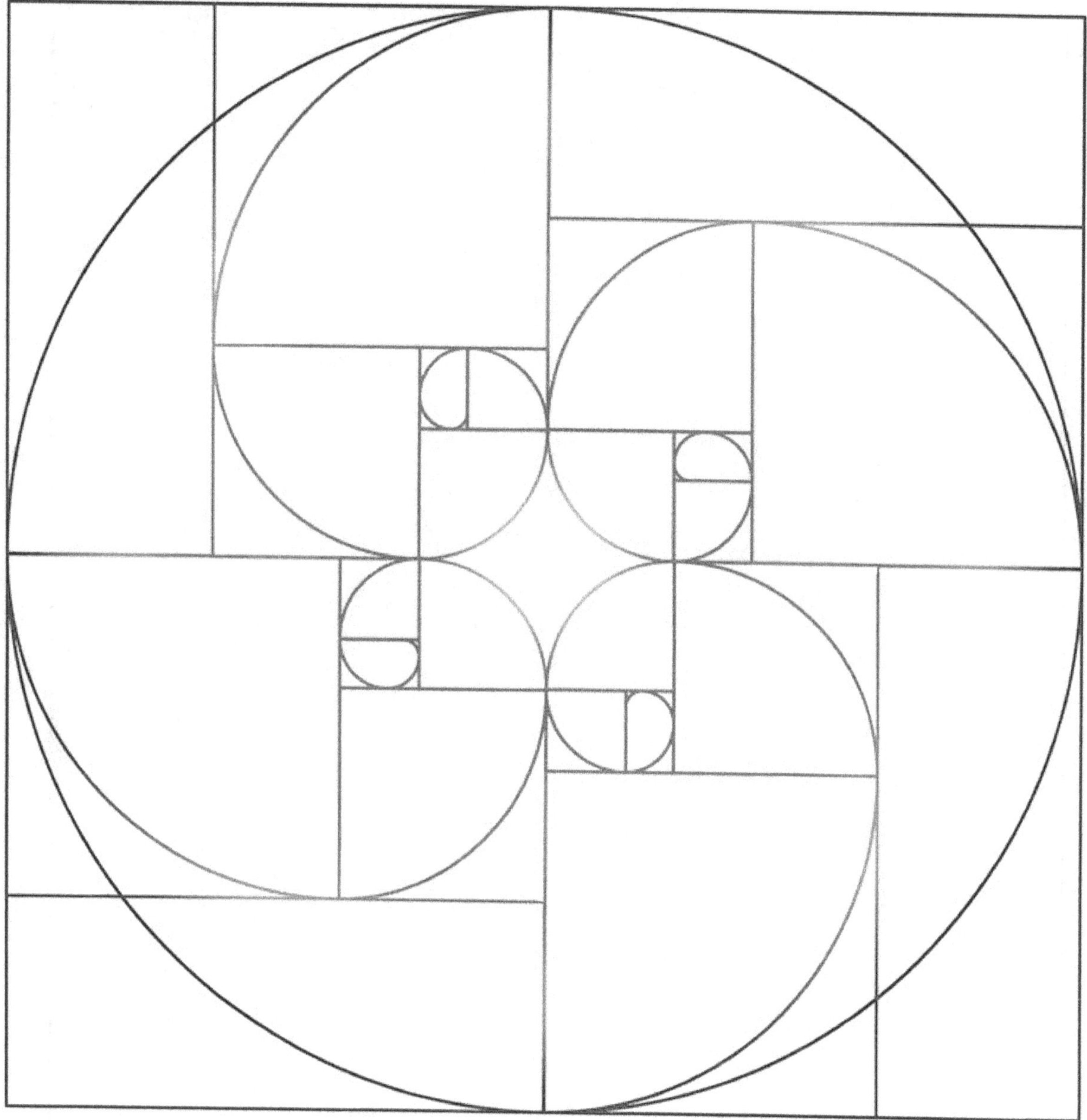

CONCLUSION

Hope you enjoyed using this journal and with its help, opened a few creative channels.

If you like this book format, please leave an honest review on Amazon or other sources.

J. Ronald Adair

Email: jradair@eltekpublishing.com Website: www.eltekpublishing.com

Other works found on Amazon by the Author/Publisher:

	"Killer" 42 (a how-to book on playing the domino game '42' at a high level) Sold on Amazon as both a paperback and Kindle book. Website: www.killer42.com
	Grandparents and parents! Save your Millennial family members. You know they are clueless in many ways. This book is THE book to help them navigate through the complexities of life! If you are a Millennial or a Gen Z'er, and wonder why you seem to be always in trouble with just daily problems, then you MUST have this book! www.clueless101.com
	Stressed out? Had enough of the demanding modern world and would like to jump off the runaway 'progress' train? This book shows you how! By applying the points presented, you too can gain control of your finances, time, family functionality, and peace of mind. This book is a humorous look at human nature, 'progress', and the many ways today's Luddite rebels are still flailing away! www.embracingluddism.com